Megan Eckman

# Everyday Embroidery

## FOR MODERN STITCHERS

50 Iron-On Designs · 15 Projects Anyone Can Make

D0999068

## stash BOOKS

*an imprint of C&T Publishing*

Text copyright © 2020 by Megan Eckman

Photography copyright © 2020 by Jeffrey Opp

Photography and artwork copyright © 2020 by C&T Publishing, Inc.

Publisher: Amy Barrett-Daffin

Creative Director: Gailen Runge

Acquisitions Editor: Roxane Cerda

Managing Editor: Liz Aneloski

Editor: Katie Van Amburg

Technical Editor / Illustrator: Linda Johnson

Cover/Book Designer: April Mostek

Production Coordinator: Zinnia Heinzmann

Production Editor: Jennifer Warren

Photo Assistant: Kaeley Hammond

Cover photography by Estefany Gonzalez and Jeffrey Opp

Instructional and subjects photography by Jeffrey Opp; lifestyle photography by Estefany Gonzalez of C&T Publishing, Inc., unless otherwise noted

Published by Stash Books, an imprint of C&T Publishing, Inc., P.O. Box 1456, Lafayette, CA 94549

All rights reserved. No part of this work covered by the copyright hereon may be used in any form or reproduced by any means—graphic, electronic, or mechanical, including photocopying, recording, taping, or information storage and retrieval systems—without written permission from the publisher. The copyrights on individual artworks are retained by the artists as noted in *Everyday Embroidery for Modern Stitchers*. These designs may be used to make items for personal use only and may not be used for the purpose of personal profit. Items created to benefit nonprofit groups, or that will be publicly displayed, must be conspicuously labeled with the following credit: "Designs copyright © 2020 by Megan Eckman from the book *Everyday Embroidery for Modern Stitchers* from C&T Publishing, Inc." Permission for all other purposes must be requested in writing from C&T Publishing, Inc.

Attention Teachers: C&T Publishing, Inc., encourages the use of our books as texts for teaching. You can find lesson plans for many of our titles at ctpub.com or contact us at ctinfo@ctpub.com or 800-284-1114.

We take great care to ensure that the information included in our products is accurate and presented in good faith, but no warranty is provided, nor are results guaranteed. Having no control over the choices of materials or procedures used, neither the author nor C&T Publishing, Inc., shall have any liability to any person or entity with respect to any loss or damage caused directly or indirectly by the information contained in this book. For your convenience, we post an up-to-date listing of corrections on our website (ctpub.com). If a correction is not already noted, please contact our customer service department at ctinfo@ctpub.com or P.O. Box 1456, Lafayette, CA 94549.

Trademark (™) and registered trademark (®) names are used throughout this book. Rather than use the symbols with every occurrence of a trademark or registered trademark name, we are using the names only in the editorial fashion and to the benefit of the owner, with no intention of infringement.

Library of Congress Cataloging-in-Publication Data

Names: Eckman, Megan Marie, 1987- author.

Title: Everyday embroidery for modern stitchers : 50 iron-on designs : 15 projects anyone can make / Megan Eckman.

Description: Lafayette, CA : Stash Books, an C&T Publishing, Inc., [2020]

Identifiers: LCCN 2020017590 | ISBN 9781617459320 (trade paperback) | ISBN 9781617459337 (ebook)

Subjects: LCSH: Embroidery--Patterns.

Classification: LCC TT771 .E26 2020 | DDC 746.44/041--dc23

LC record available at https://lccn.loc.gov/2020017590

Printed in China

10 9 8 7 6 5 4 3 2 1

## DEDICATION

*For my grandma, who taught my brother and me how to embroider,*

*and for my dad, who bought me my one and only cross-stitch.*

## Acknowledgments

I couldn't have made this book without help from a whole slew of people. A huge round of thanks to Katie Van Amburg, Liz Aneloski, Roxane Cerda, Estefany Gonzalez, Kaeley Hammond, Zinnia Heinzmann, Linda Johnson, April Mostek, Gailen Runge, and Jennifer Warren. You all have the patience of saints.

I need to thank Sonia Lyne of Dandelyne for providing such adorable mini hoops for these projects. Big thanks also to Jenny Hart of Sublime Stitching for making amazing embroidery floss, and to Rachael Derbin, who was kind enough to go through her closet and find a jean jacket for me.

Most especially, a big thank-you to my partner in all things, Jeffrey Opp, for being my photographer, cheerleader, coffee maker, and shoulder to cry on.

# CONTENTS

## EMBROIDER YOUR APPAREL   30

## LET YOUR CRAFT FLAG FLY   46   *continued* ⟶

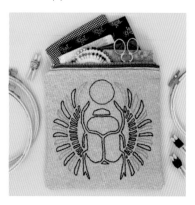

# INTRODUCTION

When you grow up in the Midwest, you can't help but be practical. Fools don't survive many North Dakota winters. My grandma, being very practical, taught my younger brother and me embroidery one rainy day at my grandparents' lake place. I'd like to say it was to pass on her skills, but really it was to prevent us from getting on our grandpa's nerves.

Twenty years later, I stumbled back into embroidery during an artistic burnout period. I needed something relaxing, something creative, to take my mind off my perceived failures. That late-night embroidery project inexplicably spawned a business that has grown for over a decade now.

When I was asked to write this book, I panicked. I wasn't crafty! Yes, I had just bought my first sewing machine, but it's not like I knew how to use it. I didn't have tubs in my closet housing glue guns, pom-poms, and googly eyes. Heck, I didn't even own glue other than wood glue. How could I write a crafting book about embroidery?

And then it hit me: I could write a crafting book for people like me. People who are just dipping their toe into the crafty water. People who are practical and don't want to embroider a cozy for their toaster. People who want a project they can finish in a day or a weekend, not one that will fill a season. So I started making a list of all the cool projects I'd always wanted to do but didn't think I could. And then I engineered them to be approachable, practical, and, most of all, awesome.

I hope you enjoy this book! If this is your first foray into crafting and embroidery, don't panic. I've got your back. This book is divided into different sections so you can pick and choose which area of your life needs a little embroidery. All of the projects are designed to be customizable, which means you can decide which design you like best for each. I included style notes for each project to show you how I got the finished design, but you should feel free to use whatever colors you want. Since there are many more design options than there are projects, I hope you feel like you can get creative and have a blast!

# EMBROIDERY BASICS

Embroidery is such a great craft because you need so little to start. I'm all about minimalist supplies when it comes to stitching, so don't fret about filling a tub in your crafting closet now that you have this book.

**To embroider all of the projects in this book, you'll only need a few tools:**

**1** Fabric (linen, shot cotton, chambray)

**2** Embroidery floss

**3** Chalk pencil*

**4** Water-soluble pencil* (such as STABILO ALL aquarellable pencil)

**5** Water-soluble fabric-marking pen* (such as Clover Water Soluble Marker)

**6** Scissors

**7** Wash-Away Stitch Stabilizer (from C&T Publishing)

**8** Embroidery needles

**9** Embroidery hoops

**10** Mini embroidery hoop kits (by Dandelyne)

**11** Tear-Perfect Maker Tape* by Judy Gauthier (from C&T Publishing)

*Note: The indicated tools are also used for sewing. See Sewing Basics (page 26) for the other sewing tools needed.*

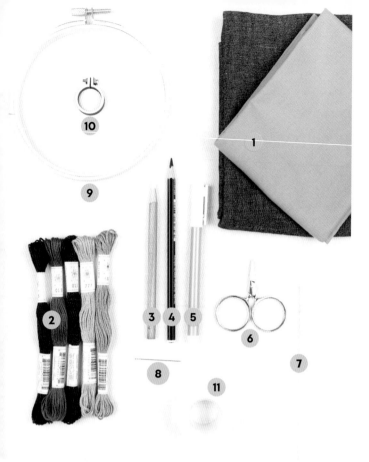

**Tip** I will mention the one caveat of using fabric from Spoonflower. Due to the way the fabric is printed, the color only appears on one side. Be aware of the white wrong sides while thinking of your projects. If all of your fabric choices have white wrong sides, it can get tricky when you layer pieces.

# Embroidery Tools

## 1 FABRIC

I'm all about simplicity when I make things, which is why I tend to shy away from fancy fabrics. I prefer natural fabrics with a loose weave that can take a bit of a stitching beating from me, because I'm always making a few mistakes in every project. My personal favorites are linens, shot cottons, chambrays, and denims, but you're welcome to use your own favorites.

I encourage you to find fabric at your local fabric shop because they often carry the coolest stuff. You can also check out Spoonflower (spoonflower.com). This online marketplace allows independent designers to sell their patterns on many different types of fabric, from cotton to spandex to everything in between.

## 2 EMBROIDERY FLOSS

Every stitcher not only has their favorite brand of embroidery floss but also their favorite number of strands with which to sew. If you're new to embroidery, you should experiment with a range of floss brands, from silky COSMO to mainstay DMC to buttery-soft Sublime Stitching. You'll also want to try stitching with different numbers of strands. If you want a delicate look, try two strands. If you want a chunky, bold look, use all six. For this book, I usually used four strands of Sublime Stitching floss to embroider each project.

## 3 CHALK PENCIL

Chalk pencils work great for transferring designs onto dark fabrics, where the water-soluble marker can't be seen. Simply brush or wash the lines away when you are done embroidering, following the directions for Preparing Embroidered Fabric for the Next Step (page 25).

## 4 WATER-SOLUBLE PENCIL

These pencils write on every surface and are much less greasy than a grease pencil. I like to use these over the water-soluble marker on fabrics that tend to cause the marker to bleed. *But be warned:* This pencil doesn't wash out with water. The lines are permanent on fabric.

## 5 WATER-SOLUBLE FABRIC-MARKING PEN

This water-soluble marker helps transfer designs onto fabric. The ink will disappear when you soak the finished embroidery in cool water. Be sure to test out your marker on a scrap of fabric before you go full steam into your project.

When you're done stitching, simply wash out the pen lines, following the directions for Preparing Embroidered Fabric for the Next Step (page 25).

## 6 SCISSORS

Find some cute embroidery scissors—and buy two pairs! Someone will inevitably borrow one and forget to give it back.

## 7 WASH-AWAY STITCH STABILIZER

These 8½″ × 11″ (21.6 × 27.9 cm) sheets (from C&T Publishing) make transferring designs easy, especially for darker fabrics. They have an adhesive backing so they stay in place while you stitch, but they aren't too sticky that they can't be easily repositioned. You can use the stitch stabilizer sheets by following the directions for The Tracing Method (page 15).

When you're done stitching, wash away the stabilizer sheet following the directions for Preparing Embroidered Fabric for the Next Step (page 25).

## 8 EMBROIDERY NEEDLES

Embroidery needles come in a wide variety of sizes, but all of them have a bigger eye than other needle types to fit embroidery floss. Sizes are numerical, with the higher numbers representing smaller, thinner needles. I prefer size 4 needles, but you can play around and see what works best for you.

## 9 EMBROIDERY HOOPS

Embroidery hoops come in all sorts of sizes and shapes. And while you don't have to use an embroidery hoop at all, I highly recommend it. Not only does it help the stitching lie flat but it also makes it easier to hold your work.

An embroidery hoop has two parts: an inner hoop and an outer hoop. The outer hoop has an adjustable sizing pin for tightening the fabric. You can use whatever size hoop you like, so long as your fabric is big enough to accommodate it. Personally, I love 5″ (12.7 cm) and 8″ (20.3 cm) hoops. For each project in this book, I'll share what hoop size I use, but you're welcome to use whichever size you prefer.

## 10 MINI EMBROIDERY HOOP KITS

These mini embroidery hoop kits (by Dandelyne) are just the cutest things ever and come in a variety of sizes. They're sturdier than normal embroidery hoops because they're laser-cut out of wood and come with a solid inner piece. Once you try these, you'll suddenly find tons of uses for them.

## 11 TEAR-PERFECT MAKER TAPE

Tape is a great way to temporarily hold iron-on transfer paper in place while you're deciding where you want to position your design. Tear-Perfect Maker Tape by Judy Gauthier (from C&T Publishing) tears easily and comes off fabric easily as well.

# How to Transfer a Design

You can use the following instructions to transfer all designs in this book.

Since we all like to have options, this book gives you several ways to transfer the embroidery designs. If you choose to use the iron-on method, you'll use the transfer-paper pullout in this book. If you choose to use the tracing method, the designs are available at **tinyurl.com/11385-patterns-download** for you to print out.

## PREPARE YOUR FABRIC

While it's my least favorite part of the process, ironing your fabric is key to your success. Lightly iron your fabric of choice to smooth out any wrinkles. Then you can choose your transfer method: either ironing or tracing.

> **Tip** If you have tough wrinkles, use a spray bottle to mist your fabric until it's damp. Then let it sit for 5–10 minutes. (I know it's hard to wait, but the moisture needs to relax the fibers in the fabric.)
>
> After 5–10 minutes have passed, set the iron to the proper heat level and start to iron, pulling the iron and the fabric toward you. This will flatten out the wrinkles before the iron gets to them, allowing you to make a nice, flat press.

## THE IRON-ON METHOD

**1.** Cut out your chosen iron-on transfer pattern from the pullout, making sure to leave at least ¼″ (6 mm) of extra space all around it. *Note:* Do not include the pattern label or it will transfer to your project as well. ⟶

**2.** Set the iron to a high heat, making sure it won't mist or steam while you're using it. With the fabric right side up, iron the fabric for 4–5 seconds to preheat it.

**3.** Place your transfer pattern wrong side down on the fabric. Press the pattern with the iron for 10–12 seconds. You can glide the iron to cover the entire pattern, but be sure the pattern doesn't shift or else the transfer image will blur. ⟶

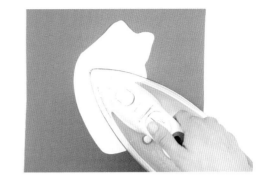

**4.** Check the darkness of the transfer by lifting up a corner. Continue ironing if you want the design to be darker.

*Note: The transfers in this book can be used several times, but they will grow fainter with each use. The transferred ink will fade with washing but won't entirely disappear. Don't worry, though, because I designed the pattern lines thin enough to be easily covered by your stitching.*

## THE TRACING METHOD

**1.** Because the pullout designs are provided as iron-on transfers, the motifs are reversed for that method to work properly. Correctly oriented patterns needed for tracing are provided for you online (see How to Transfer a Design, previous page). Once you have chosen the design you want, print it out and work from that copy for tracing. In some instances you may be able to print directly onto the stabilizer, tracing paper, or prepared fabric. Read the manufacturer instructions for your specific product. If not, use the printed copy and proceed to Step 2.

**2.** Place the stitch stabilizer, tracing paper, or fabric (if it's light colored) over the desired pattern motif. Use a water-soluble marker or chalk pencil to trace the design onto the stitch stabilizer, tracing paper, or fabric. You may want to use a brightly lit window or a lightbox to make tracing easier. ⟶

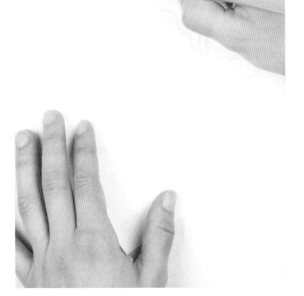

**3.** Follow one of the following methods based on what you are tracing onto.

**If using stitch-stabilizer sheets,** peel off the backing paper and attach the adhesive sheet right to the fabric.

**If using tracing paper,** gently tape it in place on the fabric. Once you have a few stitches done, it will stay secure.

**If drawing right onto the fabric,** you're ready to start embroidering.

# Before You Start Stitching

**1.** Unscrew and separate the 2 parts of the embroidery hoop. Place the fabric over the inner hoop, centering the transferred pattern. Position the outer ring on top of the fabric and push it down firmly. ————————————➤

**2.** Gently pull the fabric at each side, tightening the pin on the outer hoop as you go, until the fabric is taut. Make sure you don't pull the fabric so tight that it stretches.

**3.** Thread the needle with 24″ (61 cm) of however many strands of embroidery floss you're using. (I normally use 4 strands.) Pull the floss through about one-third of the way. Make a knot at the longer end of the floss. You can make a double knot, or you can wind the embroidery floss around your index finger 3 times and roll it off with your thumb, twisting the floss and pulling the needle-side floss as you go. ————➤

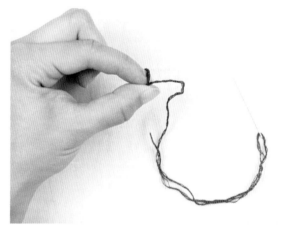

**4.** Embroider the design using either the stitches I suggest for the projects (pages 114–126) or which-ever ones you like. (When I teach a class, I always tell people that I'm not coming to their house later to check what stitches they used. So feel free to get creative!) ————————➤

**Note:** *You can use whatever size embroidery hoop you prefer for these projects. If you use a hoop smaller than the pattern, you'll have to move it around a few times as you're stitching the design. To do this, simply loosen the pin, take off the outer hoop, and move the inner hoop to the next spot. Press the outer hoop back down and retighten the pin.*

**5.** To tie off the embroidery floss, pass the needle under a nearby stitch on the back side of the fabric. Leave a little loop as you pull the floss through, and pass the needle back through that loop, pulling it tight. (I do this twice to ensure the first knot won't come undone.) Weave the needle through a few nearby stitches and cut off the excess.

# Embroidery Stitches

## RUNNING STITCH

It's always best to start easy, and it doesn't get any easier than the running stitch. Think of this stitch as if you were sewing confetti.

**1.** Come up through the fabric at the start of a short pattern line. Go down again at the end of the line, making a stitch about ¼″ (6 mm) long.

**2.** Repeat as needed, jumping around under the fabric to the start of the next pattern line.

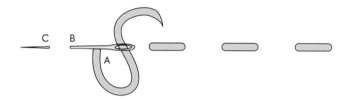

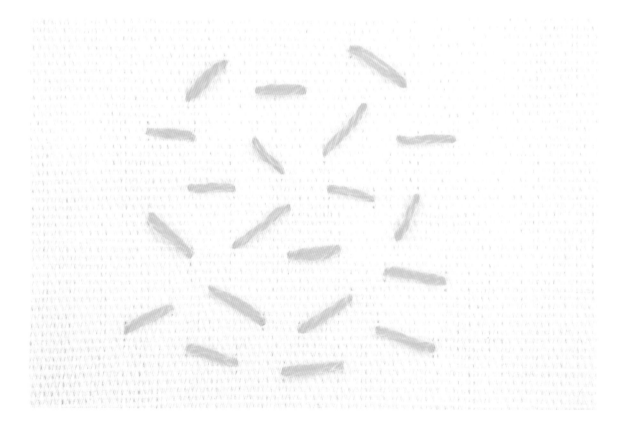

## BACKSTITCH

Sometimes you just want a clean, straight line. For that, you'll love the backstitch.

**1.** Start with a running stitch. Under the fabric, jump ahead ¼" (6 mm) on the pattern line and come up. Go back down the same hole where the running stitch ended. Now you have 2 running stitches end to end.

**2.** Come up again at the far end of the second stitch and continue to make another running stitch.

**3.** Repeat these steps, stitching forward and backward, until you have covered the pattern line. Once you get good at this stitch, you can combine the down and up steps into 1 motion.

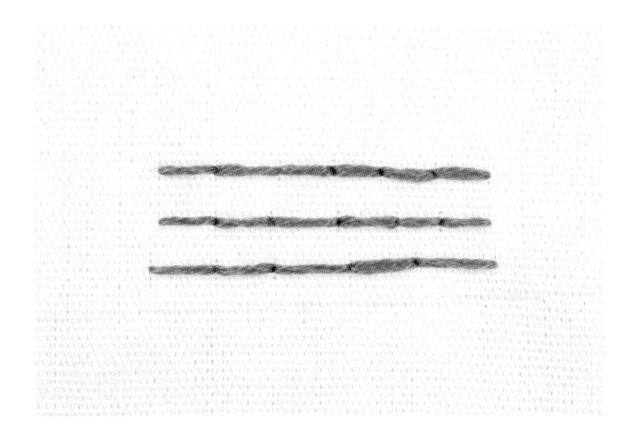

## SPLIT STITCH

Nothing beats a nice curve, and split stitches are perfect for those.

**1.** Start with a running stitch; then come back up halfway through the last stitch. The needle will come up between the threads. (Since I use 4 strands to sew, my needle has 2 strands of floss to one side and 2 to the other.)

**2.** Go back down through the fabric ¼″ (6 mm) further along the pattern line, making a second running stitch. Repeat this until you have covered the pattern line. Like the backstitch, once you get comfortable with this stitch, you can combine the down and up steps into 1 motion.

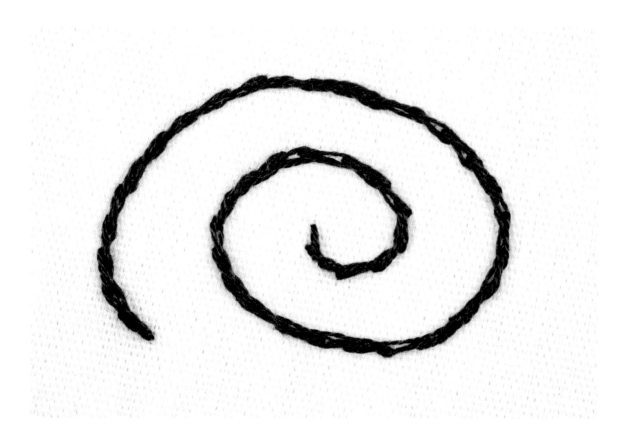

## STEM STITCH

This stitch is great for curving lines, and it's almost identical to a split stitch. The only difference is that you come up *beside* the floss instead of splitting it.

**1.** Start with a running stitch. Come back up through the fabric on one side of the halfway point of the last stitch. Go back down through the fabric about ¼″ (6 mm) further along the pattern line, making a second running stitch.

**2.** Repeat this, coming up on one side of the middle of the last stitch, until you have covered the pattern line. You'll work at a slight diagonal across the pattern line and always keep to the same side of your stitches.

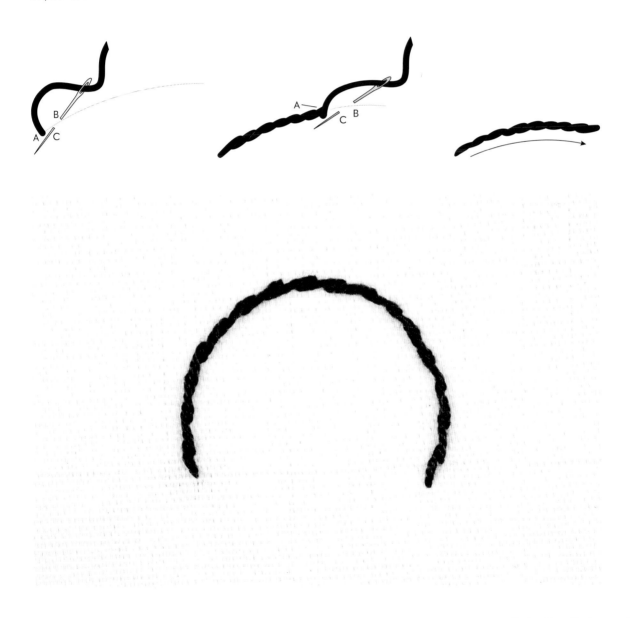

There are 2 ways to do this stitch: the traditional way and the "cheating" way. Pick whichever one you like best.

To complete the stitch in the traditional way, start by coming up from underneath the fabric. Insert the needle right next to where you came up; then pass the tip of it down under the fabric and back up ¼″ (6 mm) ahead on the pattern line. As you pull the needle through, catch the loop of the floss on it. Don't pull too tightly. You want the loop to be a little loose as it sits on the fabric. Insert the needle right next to where you came up; then pass the tip of it down under the fabric and back up ¼″ (6 mm) ahead on the pattern line. Again, make sure the needle catches the loop of floss. Continue and repeat.

If that is a bit intimidating, you can do it the cheating way, going back-ward. Sew a small running stitch (**D** in the diagram at right). Come up ¼″ (6 mm) ahead of the stitch on the pattern line and pass the needle under the first stitch but not through the fabric. Pull the floss tight. Go back down the same hole you just came up. Basically, you're hooking the floss around the running stitch. Come up ¼″ (6 mm) ahead on the pattern line and pass the needle through the bottom of the last stitch, hooking the floss again. Pull tight and go back down the hole you started the stitch in. Continue and repeat.

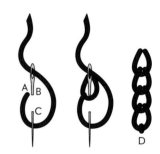

## SATIN STITCH

Bold is beautiful, and it doesn't get bolder than satin stitch.

Start at the top or bottom of the area you're filling, and make a running stitch that stretches across the entire area from left to right. Jump back to the left side under the fabric and make another running stitch just above or below the first. Repeat this until the area is filled in completely.

If this feels too intimidating, I have a trick. Start by outlining the area you want to fill with backstitches. These stitches act like a mini corral for the satin stitches so you don't have to worry about perfect edges. Then you can satin stitch between the backstitches.

## FRENCH KNOT

You can do this! I avoided this stitch for years and now I wish I'd known how easy it was.

**1.** You'll need both hands to do this stitch, so set your hoop on a table or in your lap. Come up where you want the knot. With your non-needle hand, hold the floss a few inches above the fabric and pull the floss taut. Place the needle in front of the floss and wind the floss around it twice. Keep the needle still for this, wrapping with the floss instead, but also keep the floss taut so it doesn't fall off the end of the needle.

**2.** Reinsert the tip of the needle next to, but *not into*, the hole you originally came up. Keep the needle steady with just the tip through the fabric while you give the floss a downward tug with your non-needle hand. This will coil the floss. Push the needle through the fabric and pull the floss with it. You should now have a nice little knot.

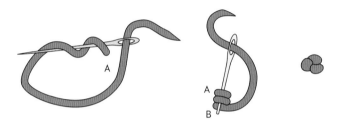

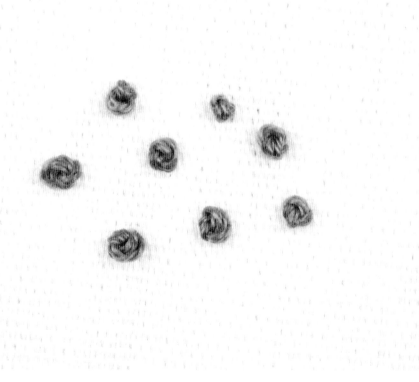

# Preparing Embroidered Fabric for the Next Step

## IF YOU USED THE IRON-ON TRANSFER METHOD

1. Mist the fabric until damp and let it sit for 10 minutes.

2. Set the iron to medium heat and gently press the fabric to get rid of wrinkles caused by the embroidery hoop.

3. Lay the embroidered fabric on a flat surface and leave it to finish drying naturally.

## IF YOU USED THE TRACING METHOD

### If You Used a Stitch-Stabilizer Sheet

1. Place the embroidered fabric as flat as possible into a sink or bowl of cool water. Leave the fabric submerged for a few minutes until the wash-away stabilizer dissolves. You may need to hold the fabric under a running tap to wash away some remaining flecks of the paper. Shake off the excess water without scrunching or squeezing the fabric.

2. Lay the fabric flat on a towel and wrap the edges over the embroidery, pressing gently to help absorb more water. Let it lay flat in the towel for 5 minutes.

3. Place the embroidered fabric right side up on a dry towel and lightly iron the fabric with a medium heat. Lay the fabric on a flat surface and leave it to finish drying naturally.

### If You Used Tracing Paper

Gently tear the paper away from the stitches.

### If You Used a Water-Soluble Marker (Right on the Fabric)

1. Place the embroidered fabric as flat as possible into a sink or bowl of cool water. Leave the fabric submerged for a few minutes until the marker disappears. Shake off the excess water without scrunching or squeezing the fabric.

2. Lay the fabric flat on a towel and wrap the edges over the embroidery, pressing gently to help absorb more water. Let it lay flat in the towel for 5 minutes.

3. Place the embroidered fabric right side up on a dry towel and lightly iron the fabric with a medium heat. Lay the fabric on a flat surface and leave it to finish drying naturally.

# SEWING BASICS

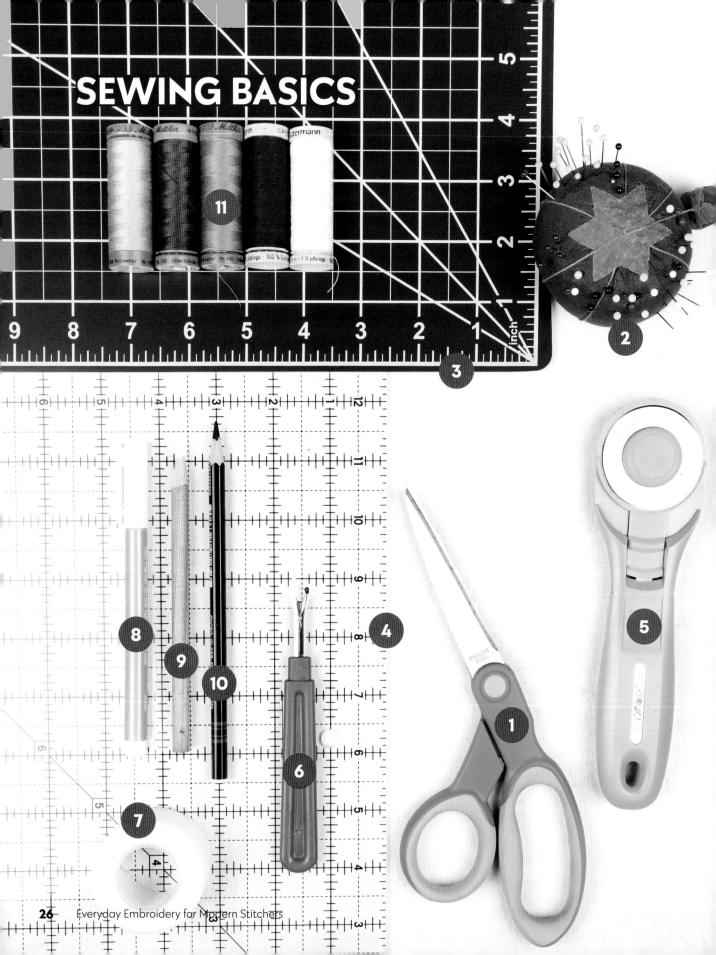

Everyday Embroidery for Modern Stitchers

I also like to keep things simple when it comes to sewing tools, so you won't see a long list here.

**To sew every project in this book, you'll need the following.**

**1** Fabric scissors

**2** Glass-head pins

**3** Cutting mat

**4** Ruler

**5** Rotary cutter

**6** Seam ripper

**7** Tear-Perfect Maker Tape* by Judy Gauthier (from C&T Publishing)

**8** Water-soluble fabric-marking pen* (such as Clover Water Soluble Marker)

**9** Chalk pencil*

**10** Water-soluble pencil* (such as STABILO ALL aquarellable pencil)

**11** Thread

**12** Sewing machine

**13** Fabric

*Note: The indicated tools are also used for embroidery. See Embroidery Basics (page 10) for the other embroidery tools needed.*

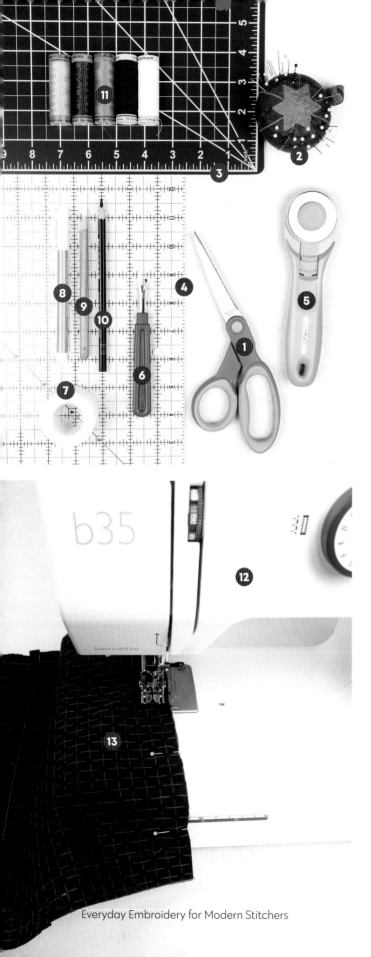

## Sewing Tools

### ❶ FABRIC SCISSORS

A committed pair of fabric scissors is a must for sewing projects. Keep a separate pair for cutting paper and other items. (My aunt once said a naughty word when I used her fabric scissors on paper. Twenty years later, I now know why.) You'll use the fabric scissors to cut stray threads and trim project corners.

### ❷ GLASS-HEAD PINS

You'll use pins to secure the fabric temporarily before and during sewing.

### ❸ ❹ ❺ CUTTING MAT, RULER, AND ROTARY CUTTER

This is the best combo for cutting fabric. The cutting mat and ruler allow for easy measuring and alignment. Plus, most mats and rulers have angle lines printed on them, which help to trim 45° corners.

Please be careful with a rotary cutter, as it's wickedly sharp. I speak from experience and a late-night trip to urgent care. Always make sure your fingers are out of the way of the blade!

### ❻ SEAM RIPPER

This tool helps you remove stitches when you've mis-stitched. Don't be afraid to use it.

### **7** TEAR-PERFECT MAKER TAPE

Tape is a great way to temporarily hold zippers or layers of fabric in place while you're preparing to sew. Tear-Perfect Maker Tape by Judy Gauthier (from C&T Publishing) tears easily and comes off fabric easily as well.

### **8** **9** **10** WATER-SOLUBLE FABRIC-MARKING PEN, CHALK PENCIL, AND WATER-SOLUBLE PENCIL

There are lots of marking tools for sewing, but I really like to use the same tools I use for the embroidery part of the project. If you keep your marks within the seam allowances, you'll never see them. Otherwise, the water-soluble marking pen and chalk pencil will come out with a little cold water. Be sure to test the marking tool on a scrap piece of fabric.

### **11** THREAD

For this book, I used Mettler Metrosene and Guenther thread. I deliberately chose contrasting colors so you could clearly see my stitches in the photos. I recommend picking subtle, complementary colors, especially if you're new to sewing, so that the stitches will be less visible. By all means, though, go full neon with the topstitching thread choices if you feel comfortable.

### **12** SEWING MACHINE

Nearly half of the projects in this book can be done without a sewing machine or can be modified to not use one. I personally love my bernette b35, and I highly recommend getting an entry-level mechanical machine if you've never owned a sewing machine. Fancier machines, obviously, work perfectly for this book, too.

One project requires a zipper foot attachment, which is a standard accessory. I also love to use a walking foot, but it's not necessary. A walking foot moves 2 or more layers of fabric through the machine at the same speed, eliminating bumps of extra fabric.

### **13** FABRIC

The sewing projects in this book require supplementary fabric for linings and backings. When considering supplementary fabrics, choose ones that will complement your embroidery fabric choice both in color and texture. My top picks are linen, canvas, chambray, and cotton. For each project, I list suggestions and tell you what I'm using.

# EMBROI

# DER YOUR APPAREL

# JEAN JACKET

Jean jackets never go out of style, so why not jazz up the one hanging in the back of your closet? Embroidery instantly transforms and personalizes your clothing, so choose a design that screams "you!"

## MATERIALS

**Jean jacket**

**Embroidery floss** ————————————

**5″ (12.7 cm) embroidery hoop**

## STYLE NOTES

**Embroidery floss:** Yellow, black, lime green

# Embroidery

**1.** Choose the Rose or another large design (see Stitch Guides, pages 114–126) to stitch onto the back of the jacket.

**2.** Transfer your chosen design, following the directions for How to Transfer a Design (page 14).

**3.** Place the jean jacket in the embroidery hoop. Stitch the embroidery however you like, or follow the Rose stitch guide (page 121).

**Note:** The smaller 5″ (12.7 cm) hoop works best here because your jacket likely has seams along the back, which are hard to press a hoop over. Just move the smaller hoop around several times as you stitch.

**4.** When you're done embroidering the design, remove the jean jacket from the hoop. Wash away any pattern marks or stabilizer, following the directions for Preparing Embroidered Fabric for the Next Step (page 25).

**5.** Let your jacket dry, and then go out and show it off to your friends!

# CANVAS SHOES

Like jean jackets, canvas shoes—from low tops to high-tops—are always stylish. Kitting them out with some embroidery is easier than you think, and it really gets people's attention.

## MATERIALS

Unlaced canvas shoes

Embroidery floss ———————————

Thimble (optional)

## STYLE NOTES

**Embroidery floss:** Pink, teal, lime green, dark pink

# Embroidery

**1.** Choose the Mini Scarab or another mini design (see Stitch Guides, pages 114–126) to stitch onto the sides of your shoes.

**2.** Transfer your chosen design, following the directions for How to Transfer a Design (page 14).

**3.** Position your design so that it's centered on the side of the shoe, or wherever you'd like to put the design.

**4.** Stitch the embroidery however you like, or follow the Mini Scarab stitch guide (page 116). If you find the canvas of the shoes a bit thick, you can use a thimble to help push the needle through the fabric.

**Tip** Try to keep the knots small for this project to avoid bumps that might rub and irritate your feet. To do this, keep a longer tail at the beginning and then go back later to tie it off with a smaller knot.

**5.** When you're done embroidering the design, wash away any pattern marks or stabilizer, following the directions for Preparing Embroidered Fabric for the Next Step (page 25).

**6.** Lace up your shoes and hit the streets. That extra bounce in your step is all thanks to embroidery!

# HALF APRON

FINISHED APRON: 27″ × 11½″ (68.6 × 29.2 cm)

Women's clothing never has enough pockets nowadays, so a half apron is perfect for crafting, cooking, or vending at a fair. The pockets are deep, the embroidery is cute, and you'll get tons of compliments from other women who wish they had your pockets.

## MATERIALS

**Main fabric:** 1 yard (91.4 cm) linen or chambray ——

**Pockets and straps:** ½ yard (45.7 cm) chambray ——

**Embroidery floss** ————————————————

**5″ (12.7 cm) embroidery hoop**

## STYLE NOTES

**Main fabric:** Linen in grass green

**Pockets and straps:** Chambray in dark blue

**Embroidery floss:** Light green, cream, orange

## CUTTING

### Main fabric

• Cut 1 rectangle
24″ × 28″ (61 × 71.1 cm).

### Pockets

• Cut 2 squares
8″ × 8″ (20.3 × 20.3 cm).

### Straps

• Cut 2 rectangles
5″ × 28″ (12.7 × 71.1 cm).

# Embroidery

**1.** Choose the Tall Crystal and Short Crystal or 2 other medium designs (see Stitch Guides, pages 114–126) to stitch onto the apron pockets.

**2.** Transfer your chosen designs onto the pocket fabric, following the directions for How to Transfer a Design (page 14).

**3.** Place one pocket in the embroidery hoop. Stitch the embroidery however you like, or follow the Tall Crystal stitch guide (page 116) and Short Crystal stitch guide (page 117).

**4.** Repeat for the second pocket.

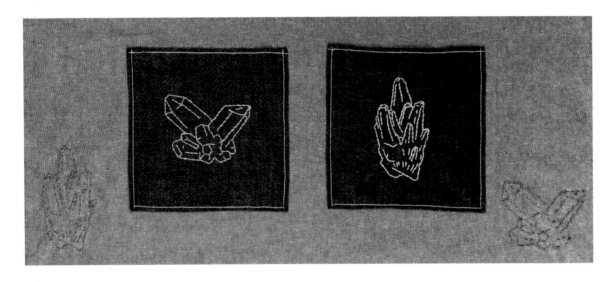

# Sewing

## PREPARATION

Remove the embroidered fabric from your hoop, wash away any pattern marks or stabilizer, and iron your fabric, following the directions for Preparing Embroidered Fabric for the Next Step (page 25).

## SEWING THE STRAPS

**1.** Fold a 5″ × 28″ (12.7 × 71.1 cm) rectangle in half the long way, right sides together, and pin. You should now have a rectangle that measures 2½″ high × 28″ wide (6.4 × 71.1 cm).

**2.** Trim an end at a 45° angle to make a pointed end. ⟶

**3.** Using a ½″ (12 mm) seam allowance, sew along the pointed end and the long side.

**4.** Trim off the excess fabric and turn the strap inside out. You may need to use a pencil or chopstick to push out the pointed end fully. Repeat for the second strap.

**5.** With your iron, press the straps so they lie flat.

## ATTACHING THE STRAPS

**1.** Fold the main fabric in half the long way with right sides together. You should now have a rectangle that measures 12″ high × 28″ wide (30.5 × 71.1 cm).

**2.** Turn the fabric so that the folded edge is along the bottom. Open the fold and insert one strap on the bottom left side, with the raw edge sticking out ½″ (12 mm). The pointed end of the strap should face inward and run along the folded edge of the main piece. Repeat with the second strap on the right side. ⟶

**3.** Close the fold and pin along the 3 open sides, marking off a 4″ (10.2 cm) gap along the top for turning.

**Tip** I use red pins to mark turning gaps. It's an easy way to remember to stop sewing.

**4.** Using a ½″ (12 mm) seam allowance, sew around the 3 sides of the rectangle, leaving the 4″ (10.2 cm) gap unstitched.

## FINISHING THE APRON

**1.** Iron the apron flat. Pin together the open section of the apron, tucking the extra fabric under and in.

**2.** Using a ¼″ (6 mm) seam allowance, topstitch around the entire apron. If you want to be bold, use a triple stitch in a contrasting color. If you want the stitching to be subtle, use a matching thread color.

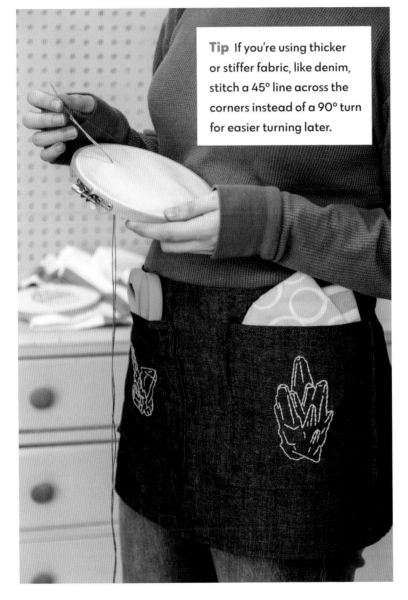

**Tip** If you're using thicker or stiffer fabric, like denim, stitch a 45° line across the corners instead of a 90° turn for easier turning later.

**5.** Trim the corners and any excess fabric around the outside, making sure you don't cut too close to your stitching—if you do, the thread will unravel. Turn the apron inside out through the 4″ (10.2 cm) gap.

**3.** Fold the top edge of a pocket under ½″ (12 mm) and pin. Using a ¼″ (6 mm) seam allowance, topstitch the top edge of the pocket. Repeat for the second pocket. ⟶

**4.** Fold the 3 raw edges of the pockets under ½″ (12 mm) and press with your iron.

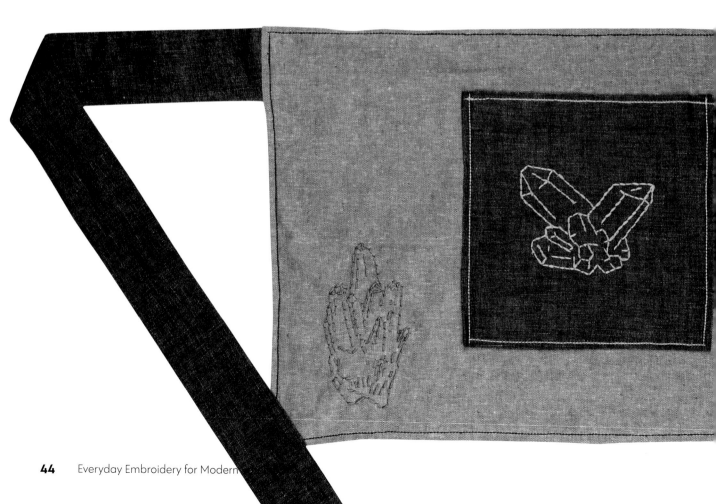

**5.** Test out your pocket placement by first pinning them in place and seeing if you like where they sit. I put mine 5½″ (14 cm) in from the sides and 1¾″ (4.4 cm) down from the top. When you're satisfied with their placement, pin them in place with 1 or 2 pins in the middle of the pockets. ⟶

**6.** Topstitch the 3 sides of the pockets.

**7.** If you want to make your apron even cooler, you can add more embroidery on the main piece, like I did with the extra crystal motifs.

**8.** Start filling your pockets with goodies—because you're done!

YOU

ROCK!

# LET CRAFT

# YOUR FLAG FLY

# LINED ZIPPER POUCH

FINISHED POUCH: 8″ × 8″  (20.3 × 20.3 cm)

Zippered pouches are a must—you can put just about anything in them.
You can stow your sewing supplies for a long bus ride, your wallet for
a night out, or your charging cables for when you travel. This 8″ × 8″
(20.3 × 20.3 cm) pouch is great for carrying everything you need for smaller
embroidery projects because a 5″  (12.7 cm) hoop slips easily inside.

**MATERIALS**

**Exterior:** ⅜ yard (34.3 cm) linen or canvas

**Lining:** ⅜ yard (34.3 cm) shot cotton

**8″ (20.3 cm) metal or plastic zipper**

**Embroidery floss**

**8″ (20.3 cm) embroidery hoop**

**Zipper foot attachment** for sewing machine

**STYLE NOTES**

**Exterior:** Spoonflower linen cotton canvas in sand

**Lining:** Shot cotton in teal

**Embroidery floss:** Black, red, teal

## CUTTING

### Exterior

- Cut 1 square 12″ × 12″ (30.5 × 30.5 cm) for the front.

- Cut 1 square 9″ × 9″ (22.9 × 22.9 cm) for the back.

### Lining

- Cut 2 squares 9″ × 9″ (22.9 × 22.9 cm).

# Embroidery

**1.** Choose the Winged Scarab or another large embroidery design (see Stitch Guides, pages 114–126) to stitch onto the pouch's exterior front.

**2.** Draw a 9″ × 9″ (22.9 × 22.9 cm) square on the exterior front fabric with chalk or a water-soluble fabric-marking pen. Transfer your chosen design where you want it within the square, following the directions for How to Transfer a Design (page 14). This ensures you're not surprised by its placement when you cut the fabric down later.

**3.** Place the fabric in the embroidery hoop. Stitch the embroidery however you like, or follow the Winged Scarab stitch guide (page 117).

# Sewing

### PREPARATION

**1.** Remove the embroidered fabric from your hoop, wash away any pattern marks or stabilizer, and iron your fabric, following the directions for Preparing Embroidered Fabric for the Next Step (page 25).

**2.** Trim the front exterior fabric to 9″ × 9″ (22.9 × 22.9 cm) to match the back exterior piece.

### SEWING THE ZIPPER

▬ **Note:** *Don't worry—you've got this! When I put my first zipper in, I was terrified. And then it turned out to be much simpler than I imagined. I even did a dance at the end and called my mother to brag. Feel free to do that as well.*

**1.** Place one exterior fabric right side up. Open the zipper so the pull is in the middle. Lay the zipper wrong side up (pull down) at the top edge of the fabric. Center the zipper so equal amounts of zipper margin go off each side, and tape the zipper in place.

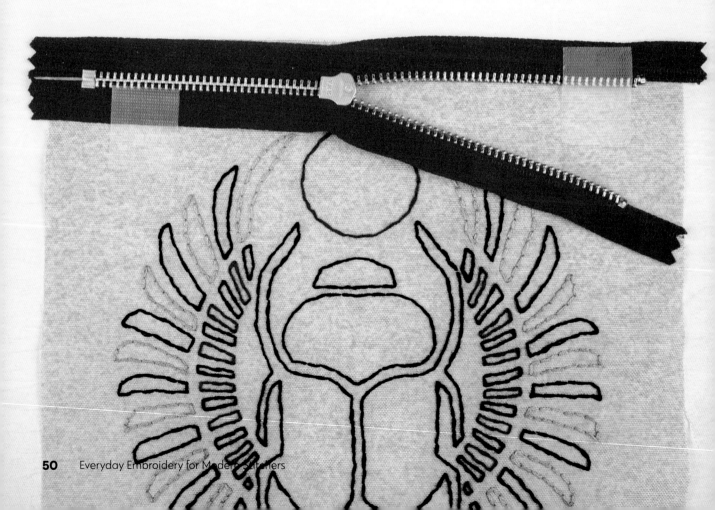

**2.** Place one of the lining pieces on top of the zipper, wrong side up, and pin all 3 layers in place along the top edge. Halfway through, move the zipper pull to the side already pinned to ensure the fabric lies flat as you pin it. Remove the tape and move the zipper pull back to the halfway point.

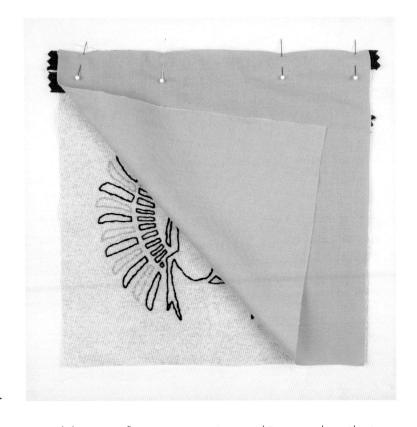

**3.** Using a ¼″ (6 mm) seam allowance and the zipper foot on your sewing machine, sew along the top edge. When you get to the zipper pull, stop with the needle down, lift the zipper foot, and move the pull to another area out of the way. Put the zipper foot back down and continue sewing all the way across.

**4.** Turn both pieces of fabric wrong sides together and press. (I know this seems like a hassle, but you want a crisp fold where the fabric meets the zipper.)

**5.** Topstitch along the fold for a polished look. It's looking awesome already! ———————→

> **Tip** *Please don't skip Step 5.* I used to think topstitching was superficial and unnecessary, but it's crucial for a pouch that lies flat.

**6.** Move the zipper pull to the center again. With the right side of the zipper and the sewn outer fabric facing up, lay the remaining outer piece of fabric on top with right sides together. Pin in place along the top edge. ———————→

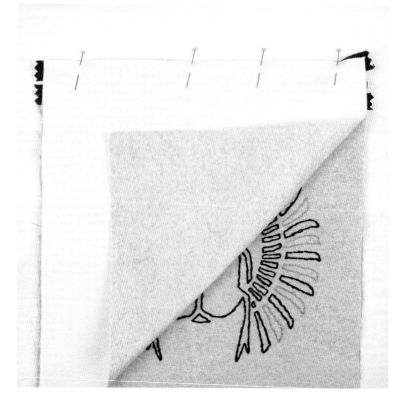

**7.** Flip the pinned fabric stack over and lay the remaining lining fabric on top with the wrong side facing upward. Pin in place along the top edge.

⟶

**8.** Repeat Steps 3–5 (pages 51 and 52) with this side of the zipper.

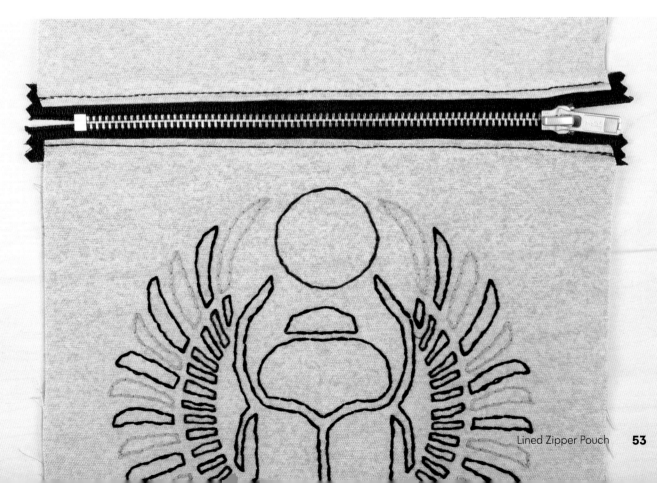

## SEWING THE POUCH

**1.** Move the zipper pull to the center of the pouch so it's out of the way. Fold the fabric pieces so that the exterior sections and the lining sections are both right sides together. Make sure to match the exterior pieces at the zipper and pin along the edges, leaving a 3″ (7.6 cm) gap along the bottom of the lining section for turning. ──────→

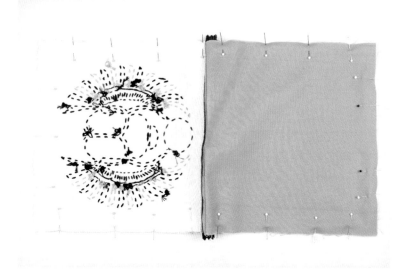

> **Tip** I use red pins to mark turning gaps. It's an easy way to remember to stop sewing.

**2.** Using a ⅜″ (10 mm) seam allowance, start on one side of the 3″ (7.6 cm) gap and straight stitch the pinned edges together.

**3.** Trim the corners at a 45° angle to remove extra fabric. This will make the turning easier and give you crisper corners. Make sure you don't cut too close to your stitching or the thread will unravel. Also trim the ends of the zipper margin that may be sticking out beyond the edges of the fabric.

## FINISHING THE POUCH

**1.** Turn the pouch inside out through the 3″ (7.6 cm) gap you left unstitched.

**2.** Pin together the open section of the lining, tucking the extra fabric under and in. Topstitch the gap closed.

**3.** Stuff the lining back inside the exterior pieces and press the pouch flat.

**4.** Fill your zipper pouch with your current embroidery project and head out to your favorite park for some outdoor stitching!

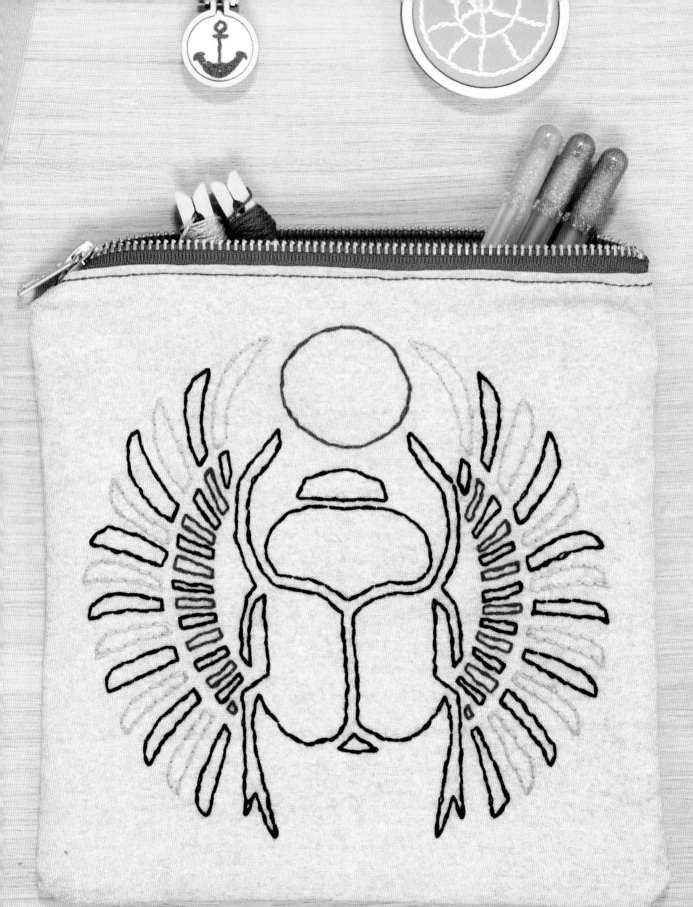

# DRAWSTRING BAG

### FINISHED POUCH: 9″ × 9″ (22.9 × 22.9 cm)

You can never have too many bags. This drawstring bag is super cute and holds quite a bit. It also works as reusable gift wrapping if you're feeling extra crafty.

## MATERIALS

**Exterior and drawstring:** ½ yard (45.7 cm) shot cotton

**Exterior accent:** ⅜ yard (34.3 cm) shot cotton

**Lining:** ⅜ yard (34.3 cm) shot cotton

**Embroidery floss**

8″ (20.3 cm) embroidery hoop

## STYLE NOTES

**Exterior and drawstring:** Shot cotton in purple

**Exterior accent:** Shot cotton in pale green

**Lining:** Shot cotton in purple

**Embroidery floss:** Green, white, teal

## CUTTING

### Exterior

- Cut 1 square 12″ × 12″ (30.5 × 30.5 cm) for the front.

- Cut 1 rectangle 9″ × 10½″ (22.9 × 26.7 cm) for the back.

### Drawstring cord

- Cut 1 rectangle 1½″ × 40″ (3.8 × 101.6 cm).

### Exterior accent

- Cut 2 rectangles 4″ × 10½″ (10.2 × 26.7 cm).

### Lining

- Cut 2 rectangles 12½″ × 10½″ (31.8 × 26.7 cm).

# Embroidery

**1.** Choose the Potted Aloe Vera or another large design (see Stitch Guides, pages 114–126) to stitch onto the pouch's exterior front.

**2.** Draw a 9″ × 10½″ (22.9 × 26.7 cm) rectangle on the exterior front fabric with chalk or a water-soluble fabric-marking pen. Transfer your chosen design where you want it within the rectangle, following the directions for How to Transfer a Design (page 14). This ensures you're not surprised by its placement when you cut the fabric down later.

**3.** Place the front fabric in the embroidery hoop. Stitch the embroidery however you like, or follow the Potted Aloe Vera stitch guide (page 126).

# Sewing

### PREPARATION

**1.** Remove the embroidered fabric from your hoop, wash away any pattern marks or stabilizer, and iron your fabric, following the directions for Preparing Embroidered Fabric for the Next Step (page 25).

**2.** Trim the front exterior fabric to 9″ × 10½″ (22.9 × 26.7 cm) to match the back exterior piece.

### SEWING THE BAG

**1.** Arrange the fabric pieces in a line on your worktable in this order: lining, exterior accent, exterior, exterior, exterior accent, lining. The 10½″ (26.7 cm) sides will be touching and the wrong sides of the fabric will be facing up. Be sure the tops of any directional prints and the embroidery face toward the lining pieces. Using a ⅜″ (10 mm) seam allowance, sew together all of the pieces to make 1 long strip.

**2.** Press the seams open. Fold the strip in half, right sides together, and match up the lining ends. Pin along the raw edges, making sure to line up the seams. Leave a 3″ (7.6 cm) gap at the center of the lining end for turning. ⟶

> **Tip** I use red pins to mark turning gaps. It's an easy way to remember to stop sewing.

**3.** Mark a 1″ (2.5 cm) opening in the center of the exterior accent piece on both the left and right sides by measuring down 1¼″ (3.2 cm) and 2¼″ (5.7 cm) from the top of the exterior accent piece. This 1″ (2.5 cm) gap on each side will be the channel for the drawstring. Mark these gaps with pins to ensure you don't sew them closed. ⟶

**4.** Using a ½″ (12 mm) seam allowance, sew along the 3 sides, remembering to leave open the 3″ (7.6 cm) gap on the lining pieces and the 1″ (2.5 cm) gaps in the exterior accent fabric.

## BOXING THE CORNERS

**1.** Starting with a lining corner, wiggle the 2 pieces of fabric apart and flatten the corner where the seams meet. Use your fingers to feel when the bottom and side seams are lined up.

**2.** Lay a ruler across the corner and line up one edge of the lining fabric with the 45° angle line on the ruler. With the seam point 1½″ (3.8 cm) into the ruler, draw a line roughly 3″ (7.6 cm) wide along the bottom of the ruler. ⟶

**3.** Pin and sew along this line. Trim off the excess fabric. You now have 1 boxed corner. ⟶

**4.** Repeat Steps 1–3 (above) for the other 3 corners.

## FINISHING THE POUCH

**1.** Turn the bag inside out through the 3″ (7.6 cm) gap you left unstitched in the lining fabric.

**2.** Pin together the open section of the lining, tucking the extra fabric under and in. Topstitch the gap closed.

**3.** Nest the lining into the exterior bag.

**4.** Pin or draw a line across the bag, connecting the top of the 1″ (2.5 cm) opening on the left side to the top of the 1″ (2.5 cm) opening on the right side. Pin or draw another line below it, connecting the bottom of the 1″ (2.5 cm) opening left to right. Extend the lines across the back of the bag as well. This will be the channel for the drawstring.

## MAKING THE DRAWSTRING CORD

**1.** Fold the short ends of the rectangle under by ½″ (12 mm), wrong sides together, and press. Fold the strip in half lengthwise, wrong sides together, and press again.

**2.** Open the fabric up, save for the short ends. Fold each raw edge to the centerline and press.

**3.** Open the fabric 1 more time. You will have 3 folds in the fabric. Refold the strip in half lengthwise, starting by folding the raw edges to the center, and press. Pin the folded edges together.

**4.** Stitch along the length of the folded fabric to finish the drawstring cord, sewing as close to the fold as you can.

**5.** Topstitch around the bag on the lines, starting at the side seams. (I like to use a triple stitch for this so that the thread really stands out.)

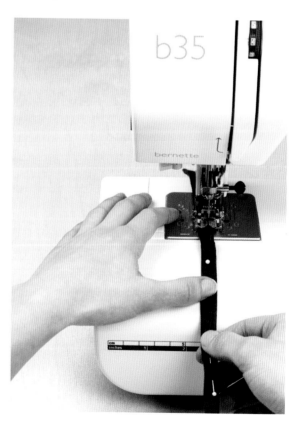

**5.** Attach a safety pin to one end of the drawstring cord and insert it into one of the openings. Shimmy the cord all the way around the bag 1½ times, passing the second hole, the hole you started in, and finally coming out the second hole.

**6.** Pop whatever you want into this handy little bag—or see whose birthday is coming up next, and find a gift that fits inside this reusable gift wrapping!

# TRAVEL COFFEE COZY

FINISHED COZY: 9″ × 2¼″ (22.9 × 5.7 cm)

Make your next coffee trip a little craftier and a lot more eco-friendly
with a felt cozy. These are super easy to sew, and they make great
gifts for friends and family because you can customize them.

| MATERIALS | STYLE NOTES |
|---|---|
| **Felt:** 1 sheet 12″ × 18″ (30.5 × 45.7 cm) ——————————— | **Felt:** Olive green |
| **Cardboard coffee insulator** from your favorite coffee shop | |
| **Embroidery floss** ——————————————————————— | **Embroidery floss:** Black, red |

# Preparation

Open the cardboard insulator, undoing the glue so it will lay flat. Notice that one end of the insulator has a straight diagonal edge and the other is slightly indented. Trace the top and bottom edge of the insulator onto the felt with a water-soluble fabric-marking pen or water-soluble pencil. Trace the straight diagonal end onto the felt and then flip the insulator over to trace that end a second time on the other side. You will now have something that looks like the arc of a rainbow on the felt.

# Embroidery

**1.** Choose the Crafter design or several mini designs (see Stitch Guides, pages 114–126) to stitch onto the felt within the marking lines.

**2.** Transfer your chosen design(s), following the directions for How to Transfer a Design (page 14).

**3.** Holding the project in your hands (I recommend skipping the embroidery hoop for this project—it can leave marks in the felt), stitch the embroidery however you like, or follow the Crafter stitch guide (page 121). ⟶

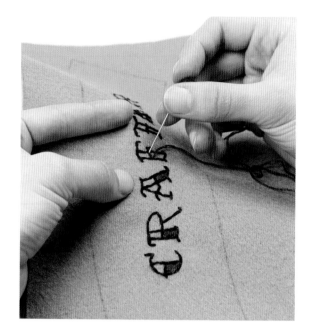

> **Tip** Test stitch on a piece of scrap felt first. Felt is easy to sew through, but its fuzzy fibers tend to swallow embroidery floss. You may want to use six strands of embroidery floss for this project to make sure your stitches stand out.

**4.** Using scissors, cut along the marking lines to cut out the cozy. ⟶

# Sewing

**1.** Fold the felt in half, wrong sides together, and pin along the short end. Triple stitch a ⅜″ (10 mm) seam along the short end. ⟶

**2.** Head out to your favorite coffee shop and treat yourself to a hot beverage. As you nestle it in your new coffee cozy, watch the barista get jealous.

# EMBROIDERED CARDS

FINISHED CARDS: 4¼″ × 5½″ (10.8 × 14 cm)

Want to up your stationery game? Add a little thread. Your friends will love receiving a mini embroidery project in their mailbox.

## MATERIALS

Card stock or Canson Mi-Teintes paper:
8½″ × 11″ (21.6 × 27.9 cm)

Embroidery floss

## STYLE NOTES

Card stock or Canson Mi-Teintes
paper: Yellow

Embroidery floss: Teal

# Preparation

Cut the card stock in
half the short way, so you
have 2 pieces measuring
5½″ high × 8½″ wide
(14 × 21.6 cm).

# Embroidery

**1.** Choose the Diamond or
another medium design (see
Stitch Guides, pages 114–126)
to stitch onto the paper.

**2.** Transfer your chosen design
onto the right-hand side of the
paper, following the directions
for How to Transfer a Design
(page 14). Tracing paper or
tracing with this paper works
best. You can use iron-on
transfers on paper, but you will
want to test it out first and be
careful not to leave the iron on
for too long.

**3.** Set the card on a cutting mat and use an embroidery needle to punch through the paper where the design lines intersect each other. Hold the paper up slightly from the mat as you punch. ⎯⎯⎯⎯⎯⎯⎯⎯⎯⎯➤

> **Tip** Embroidering on paper works best if you stretch your stitches longer and use a backstitch. I specifically chose a design with straight lines to reduce the risk of creasing the paper or punching too many holes. If you'd like to stitch a design with curved lines, punch holes along the curved lines every ¼" (6 mm), and backstitch the design.

**4.** Backstitch the embroidery using whatever colors you like, or follow the Diamond stitch guide (page 120). I recommend using 6 strands of floss to really make the design pop. Hold the paper gently as you embroider the design, using the prepunched holes for the stitches.

⎯⎯⎯⎯⎯⎯⎯⎯⎯⎯⎯⎯⎯⎯⎯➤

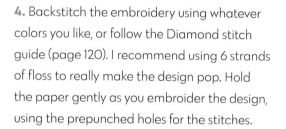

**5.** When you're done stitching, tie off the embroidery floss like normal. Fold the paper in half to finish the card.

## OPTIONAL: HANDWRITING EMBROIDERY

Add another personal touch by turning your handwriting into embroidery. Write on the card in pencil or marker and embroider over the top, punching holes every ¼" (6 mm) on the lines for a backstitch.

# BROIDERED NOTEBOO

### FINISHED NOTEBOOK: 5″ × 8¼″  (12.7 × 21 cm)

Forget doodling on your notebook cover to personalize it.
Why not try adding a little embroidery floss?

Embroidery for Modern Stitchers

## MATERIALS

**Kraft paper–covered notebook:** 8¼″ × 5″
(21 × 12.7 cm)

**Embroidery floss** ————————————

## STYLE NOTES

**Embroidery floss:** Red, green, black

# Embroidery

**1.** Choose the Cherries or another medium design (see Stitch Guides, pages 114–126) to stitch onto the notebook cover.

**2.** Transfer your chosen design onto the front of the notebook cover, following the directions for How to Transfer a Design (page 14). Ironing does not work with kraft paper, but tracing paper works well. Be sure to very lightly tape the tracing paper in place so it doesn't tear the cover. ————→

**3.** Open the notebook and set the cover on a cutting mat. Use an embroidery needle to punch through the kraft paper cover every ¼″ (6 mm) along the design lines. Hold the cover up slightly from the mat as you punch. ⟶

> **Tip** If you stitch a design with curved lines, like the Cherries, punching holes along the curved lines every ¼″ (6 mm) makes it easy to backstitch the design. You can also sew a more linear design, like the Diamond, by punching holes where the design lines intersect and using longer stitches.

**4.** Backstitch the embroidery using whatever colors you like, or follow the Cherries stitch guide (page 120). I recommend using 6 strands of floss to really make the design pop. Hold the cover gently as you embroider your design, using the prepunched holes for your stitches. Tie off the embroidery floss like normal. ⟶

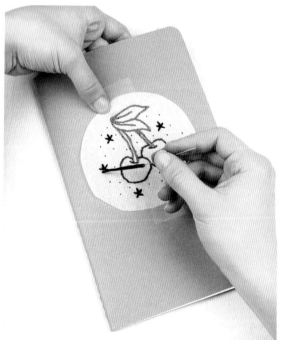

# STITCH

# ACCE

Everyday Embroidery for Modern Stitchers

# UP SOME SSORIES

# FABRIC CUFF

FINISHED CUFF: 7½″ × 2″ (19.1 × 5.1 cm)

Wonder Woman made cuffs fashionable again, so why not make a fabric one?
It won't clang on your desk, and you can wear it through airport security.

## MATERIALS

**Front fabric:** ¼ yard (22.9 cm) shot cotton ———

**Back fabric:** ⅛ yard (11.4 cm) shot cotton ———

**Fusible interfacing:** ⅛ yard (11.4 cm)

**Embroidery floss** ————————————

**5″ (12.7 cm) embroidery hoop**

**Elastic band or hair tie**

**Cool button**

## STYLE NOTES

**Front fabric:** Shot cotton in salmon

**Back fabric:** Shot cotton in blue

**Embroidery floss:** Dark blue, yellow

## CUTTING

### Front fabric

• Cut 1 square 9″ × 9″ (22.9 × 22.9 cm).

### Back fabric

• Cut 1 rectangle 3″ × 8½″ (7.6 × 21.6 cm).

### Fusible interfacing

• Cut 1 rectangle 3″ × 8½″ (7.6 × 21.6 cm).

# Embroidery

**1.** Choose the Mini Swallow or several other mini designs (see Stitch Guides, pages 114–126) to stitch onto the front of the cuff.

**2.** Draw a 2″ × 7½″ (5.1 × 19.1 cm) rectangle in the center of your front fabric piece with chalk or a water-soluble fabric-marking pen. This is the space you can embroider within. As you decide where to position your designs, remember that you'll be attaching a button 1″–2″ (2.5–5.1 cm) in from one of the short ends of the cuff. ——→

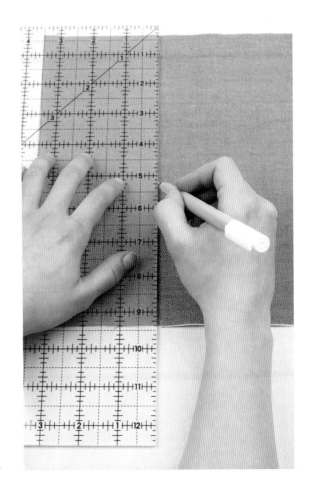

**3.** Transfer your chosen designs, following the directions for How to Transfer a Design (page 14). I transferred the swallows using the tracing method to have them fly in multiple directions.

**4.** Place the front fabric in the embroidery hoop. Stitch the embroidery however you like, or follow the Mini Swallow stitch guide (page 119). I free-stitched in the yellow running stitches to fill the space more.

# Sewing

## PREPARATION

**1.** Remove the embroidered fabric from the hoop, wash away any pattern marks or stabilizer, and iron your fabric, following the directions for Preparing Embroidered Fabric for the Next Step (page 25).

**2.** Trim the front fabric to 3″ × 8½″ (7.6 × 21.6 cm) to match the back fabric, giving your drawn rectangle a ½″ (12 mm) border on all sides.

## APPLYING THE FUSIBLE INTERFACING

**1.** Lay the front fabric wrong side up on an ironing board, and lightly pin the fusible interfacing on top of it, textured side down. The edges should all line up.

**2.** Set your iron to the steam setting, and gently touch the tip of the iron along the edges of the interfacing, just enough to make it stick slightly. ──────────────────────────→

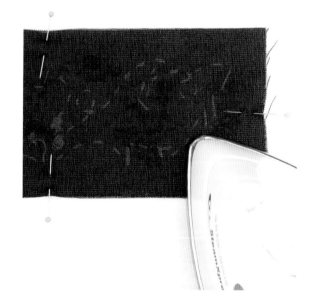

**3.** Remove the pins and cover the interfacing with a damp cloth.

**4.** Press down firmly with the iron for 10 seconds. Lift the iron and reposition it, if needed, to fully steam the entire cuff. Check to make sure the interfacing is fully fused to the fabric. If it's not, press it again.

## SEWING THE CUFF

**1.** Lay the front fabric right side up. Lay the backing fabric on top of it, right sides together. Pin around the edges, leaving a 3″ (7.6 cm) gap along one long side for turning.

> **Tip** I use red pins to mark turning gaps. It's an easy way to remember to stop sewing.

**2.** Unpin one of the short ends and put the elastic band in between the layers. Half of the elastic band will hang outside of the fabric stack. Press the 2 sides of the elastic band together so they touch, and pin the elastic band in place between the 2 layers of fabric. ⟶

**3.** Using a ½″ (12 mm) seam allowance, sew around the outside of the cuff. You may need to re-pin as you near the elastic band to hold it in place. Backing the sewing machine needle over the elastic band and stitching over it a second time will ensure it doesn't come loose. ⟶

**4.** Trim the corners at a 45° angle to remove extra fabric. This will make the turning easier and give you crisper corners. Make sure you don't cut too close to your stitching or your thread will unravel.

**5.** Turn the cuff inside out through the 3″ (7.6 cm) gap you left unstitched. You may need to use a pencil or chopstick to push out the corners fully.

**6.** Press the cuff lightly with the iron.

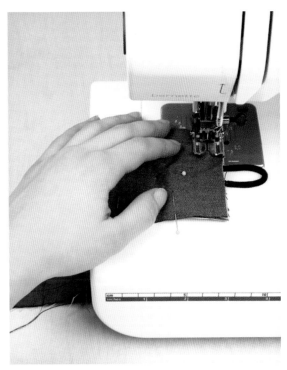

**7.** Pin together the open section of the lining, tucking the extra fabric under and in. Topstitch the gap closed.

**Note:** *If you want to hide your topstitching, you can use a thread color that matches the fabric and just stitch the gap closed. Alternatively, you can use a contrasting thread color and topstitch around the entire cuff.*

## FITTING THE CUFF

**1.** Put the cuff around your wrist and see where the loop of the elastic band touches the other side of the cuff. Mark that spot with a water-soluble fabric-marking pen or chalk pencil. ⟶

**2.** Sew the button onto the marked spot, letting it be a little loose so that the elastic band can fit under it.

**3.** Head downtown to meet your friends and wait for the compliments.

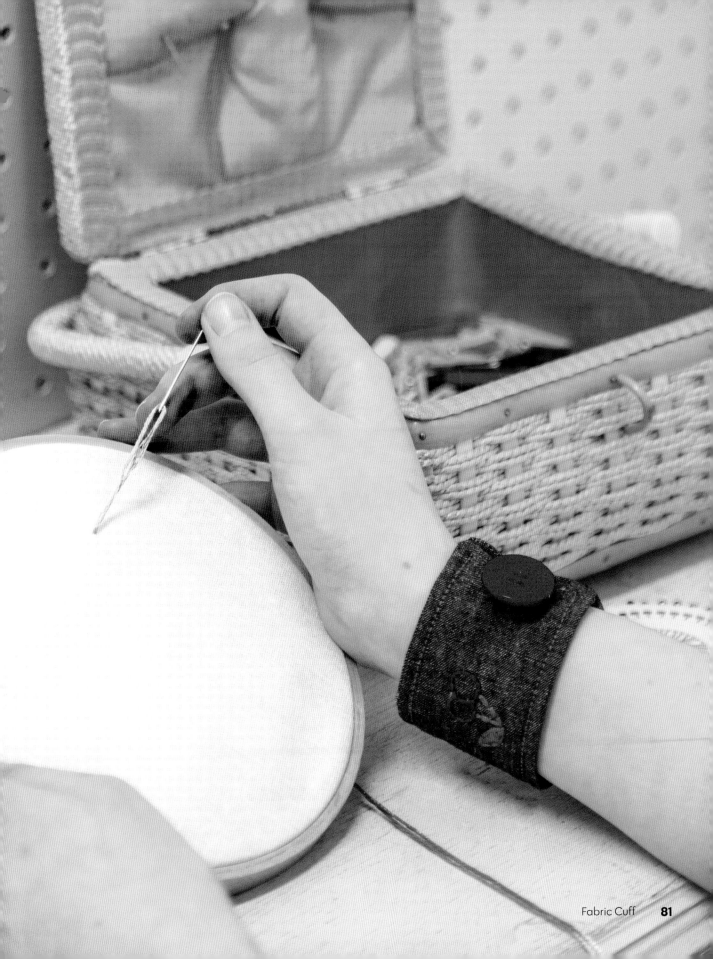

# MINI HOOP PINBACK BUTTON

FINISHED PIN: 2¼″ (5.7 cm) circle

Pinback buttons are the perfect way to subtly express your personality when you're out in public. Making one with a mini embroidery hoop adds an extra layer of cool.

**MATERIALS**

**Fabric:** 7½″ × 7½″ (19.1 × 19.1 cm) square shot cotton

**Embroidery floss**

5″ (12.7 cm) embroidery hoop

**Mini hoop kit with brooch (by Dandelyne):**
55 mm (2¼″)

**All-purpose craft glue**

**STYLE NOTES**

**Fabric:** Shot cotton in purple

**Embroidery floss:** Cream and teal

# Embroidery

**1.** Choose the Mini Skull or another mini design to fill your hoop. Refer to Mini Hoop Sizing for Mini Designs (page 107) to find the correctly sized designs for a 55 mm (2¼″) mini hoop.

**2.** Transfer your chosen design onto the fabric, following the directions for How to Transfer a Design (page 14). Be sure to place your design in the middle of the fabric so you can use the 5″ (12.7 cm) embroidery hoop to sew it.

**3.** Place the fabric in the 5″ (12.7 cm) embroidery hoop. Stitch the embroidery however you like, or follow the Mini Skull stitch guide (page 115).

### PREPARATION

Remove the embroidered fabric from the hoop, wash away any pattern marks or stabilizer, and iron your fabric, following the directions for Preparing Embroidered Fabric for the Next Step (page 25).

## MINI HOOP COMPONENTS

Each mini hoop consists of 3 major components and some hardware.

**1. Outer ring:** Made of wood or acrylic

**2. Center plate:** Thicker round disk

**3. Backing disk:** Thin round disk with a notch

The hoop will close with a screw and nut.

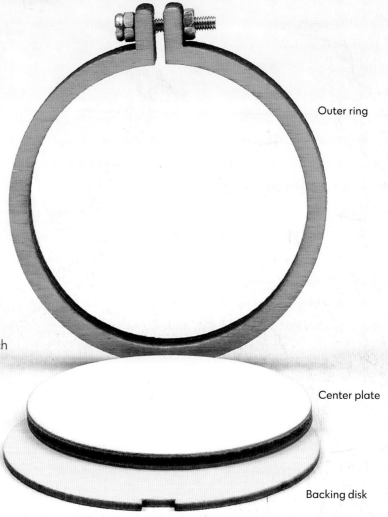

Outer ring

Center plate

Backing disk

## ASSEMBLING THE MINI HOOP

**1.** Set the outer ring of the mini hoop on top of the embroidered fabric, centering your stitched design. Draw a circle ¼" (6 mm) out from the hoop and cut along the line. ⟶

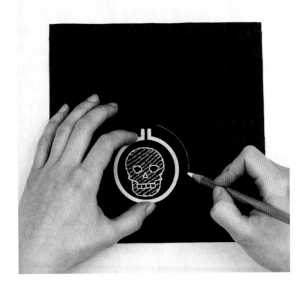

**2.** Center the fabric on the center plate of the mini hoop. Push the outer ring of the mini hoop down over the top, securing the fabric between the two. You may need to push the center plate forward a bit until the embroidered fabric is just at the front edge of the outer ring.

**3.** Flip the hoop over and apply a thin line of glue around the edge of the center plate. Push the fabric down onto the glue in a circular motion. Let the glue dry. ⟶

> **Tip** Add a little glue to the inside of the fabric as well. This will help it stay flat when you press it down.

**4.** Add glue to the backing disk, putting it right up to the edge. Position the backing disk on the back of the mini hoop with the notch at the top and press down firmly. Let the glue dry.

**5.** Put one nut on the bolt, screwing it up to the very top. Insert the bolt through the holes in the top of the mini hoop. Add the second nut to the end and screw until it's tight.

**6.** Flip the hoop over and glue the pin to the back.

**7.** Let the glue dry fully, and then pin the button to your favorite bag or jacket. You're a crafting rock star now!

## OPTIONAL: ADD A COMPLEMENTING PIN

These pins look great in all sizes, from the largest 2¼" (5.7 cm) hoop to the smallest 1" (2.5 cm) mini hoop. I couldn't help but make a smaller one to go with my skull.

# MINI HOOP NECKLACE

FINISHED NECKLACE: 1½˝ (3.8 cm) circle

Mini embroidery hoops look good everywhere, but they're especially cute as a necklace. This piece is so lightweight that you'd forget you were wearing it—if people weren't constantly complimenting you on it!

## MATERIALS

**Fabric:** 7½″ × 7½″ (19.1 × 19.1 cm) —————— square Kona Cotton

**Embroidery floss** ——————————————

**5″ (12.7 cm) embroidery hoop**

**Mini hoop kit with necklace (by Dandelyne):** 40 mm (1½″)

**All-purpose craft glue**

## STYLE NOTES

**Fabric:** Kona Cotton in white

**Embroidery floss:** Lime green, green, dark purple

# Embroidery

**1.** Choose the Mini Potted Succulent or another mini design to fill your hoop. Refer to Mini Hoop Sizing for Mini Designs (page 107) to find the correctly sized design options for a 40 mm (1.6″) mini hoop.

**2.** Transfer your chosen design onto the fabric, following the directions for How to Transfer a Design (page 14). Be sure to place your design in the middle of the fabric so you can use your 5″ (12.7 cm) embroidery hoop to sew it.

**3.** Place the fabric in the 5″ (12.7 cm) embroidery hoop. Stitch the embroidery however you like, or follow the Mini Potted Succulent stitch guide (page 123).

### PREPARATION

Remove the embroidered fabric from the hoop, wash away any pattern marks or stabilizer, and iron the fabric, following the directions for Preparing Embroidered Fabric for the Next Step (page 25).

## ASSEMBLING THE MINI HOOP

**1.** Follow the instructions for Mini Hoop Pinback Button, Assembling the Mini Hoop, Steps 1–4 (pages 85 and 86).

**2.** Put one nut on the bolt, screwing it up to the very top. Insert the bolt through the first hole in the top of the mini hoop and slip on the necklace's jump ring. Finish sliding the bolt through the second hole in the top of the mini hoop. Add the second nut to the end and screw until it's tight. ——————————————→

**3.** Wear your new necklace to a party and see how many people ask you where you bought it!

# CREATE A

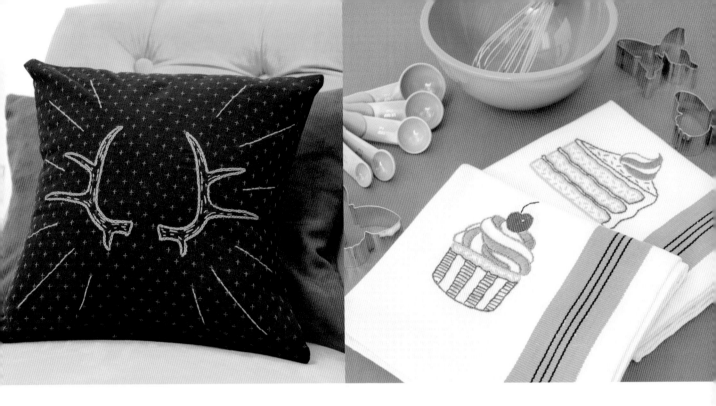

# CRAFTY HOME

# TEA TOWELS

FINISHED TEA TOWEL: 17″ × 30″  (43.2 × 76.2 cm)

Your grandma likely had a large collection of tea towels, but that doesn't mean they can't be cool. It's all a matter of picking the right design. Instead of day-of-the-week cats, we're going to make a cupcake and a slice of cake.

## MATERIALS

**Toweling fabric:** 1¾ yards (1.7 m) ——————

**Embroidery floss** ——————

5″ (12.7 cm) embroidery hoop

## STYLE NOTES

**Toweling fabric:** White with teal stripes

**Embroidery floss:** Pink, yellow, black, teal

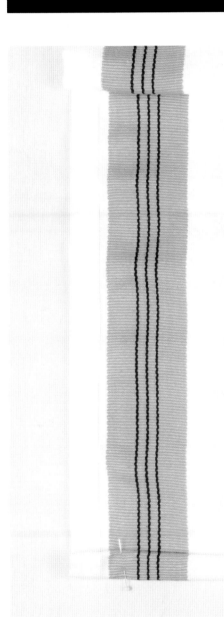

## CUTTING

**Toweling fabric**

- Cut in half to yield 2 equal rectangles
  ⅞ yard (80 cm) long.

# Sewing

## PREPARATION

**1.** Fold up the bottom edge ½″ (12 mm) twice, and pin in place. Using a ⅜″ (10 mm) seam allowance, sew along the edge to create a finished edge.

**2.** Repeat for the other end of the towel.

# Embroidery

**1.** Choose the Cupcake and Cake or 2 other medium designs (see Stitch Guides, pages 114–126) to stitch onto the towels.

**2.** Transfer your chosen designs, following the directions for How to Transfer a Design (page 14).

**3.** Position the design so that it sits near the bottom edge of the towel. This way you'll see it when you hang it from your oven. You can decide whether you want it centered or off-centered, depending on the striping on your toweling.

**4.** Place the toweling in the embroidery hoop. Stitch the embroidery however you like, or follow the Cupcake stitch guide (page 121) and Cake stitch guide (page 121).

**5.** Remove the embroidered fabric from the hoop, wash away any pattern marks or stabilizer, and iron the fabric, following the directions for Preparing Embroidered Fabric for the Next Step (page 25).

**6.** Repeat for the second towel.

**7.** Hang them on your oven and pat yourself on the back while enjoying a well-deserved cupcake!

# COASTERS

**FINISHED COASTER: 4″ × 4″ (10.2 × 10.2 cm)**

Protect your furniture and decorate it at the same time! These adorable coasters tell your guests you're crafty *and* responsible. Coasters also make great housewarming presents for your friends and family. Bonus points if you send the kids off to college with them.

## MATERIALS

**Front fabric:** ¼ yard (22.9 cm) Kona Cotton ———

**Backing fabric:** ¼ yard (22.9 cm) Kona Cotton ———

**Felt:** 1 sheet 12″ × 18″ (30.5 × 45.7 cm)

**Embroidery floss** ————————————————

**5″ (12.7 cm) embroidery hoop**

## STYLE NOTES

**Front fabric:** Kona Cotton in white

**Backing fabric:** Kona Cotton in dark gray

**Embroidery floss:** Teal, dark green, pink, and dark gray

## CUTTING

### Front fabric

• Cut 4 squares 8″ × 8″ (20.3 × 20.3 cm).

### Backing fabric

• Cut 4 squares 5″ × 5″ (12.7 × 12.7 cm).

### Felt

• Cut 4 squares 4¼″ × 4¼″ (10.8 × 10.8 cm).

# Embroidery

**1.** Choose the Green Succulent, Pink Succulent, Teal Succulent, and Gray Succulent or 2–4 other medium designs (see Stitch Guides, pages 114–126) to stitch onto the coasters.

**2.** Transfer your chosen designs, following the directions for How to Transfer a Design (page 14).

**3.** Place the front fabric in the embroidery hoop. Stitch the embroidery however you like, or follow the Green Succulent stitch guide (page 124), Pink Succulent stitch guide (page 124), Teal Succulent stitch guide (page 125), and Gray Succulent stitch guide (page 125).

# Sewing

## PREPARATION

**1.** Remove the embroidered fabric from the hoop, wash away any pattern marks or stabilizer, and iron the fabric, following the directions for Preparing Embroidered Fabric for the Next Step (page 25).

**2.** Trim the front fabric to 5″ × 5″ (12.7 × 12.7 cm) to match the backing fabric.

## SEWING THE COASTER

**1.** Stack the embroidered front fabric on top of the backing fabric, right sides together. Center the felt on top of the embroidered front fabric.

**2.** Pin together the stack, marking a 3″ (7.6 cm) gap along one side for turning. ⟶

> **Tip** I use red pins to mark turning gaps. It's an easy way to remember to stop sewing.

**3.** Using a ½″ (12 mm) seam allowance, sew around the coaster, leaving the 3″ (7.6 cm) gap unstitched.

**4.** Trim the corners at a 45° angle to remove extra fabric. This will make the turning easier and give you crisper corners. Make sure you don't cut too close to the stitching or the thread will unravel. Trim excess fabric from the 3 stitched sides as well. ⟶

**5.** Turn the coaster inside out through the 3″ (7.6 cm) gap you left unstitched. You may need to use a pencil or chopstick to push out the corners fully.

**6.** Pin together the open section of the lining, tucking the extra fabric under and in.

**7.** Topstitch the gap closed.

■ **Note:** *If you want to hide your topstitching, you can use a thread color that matches the fabric and just stitch the gap closed. Alternatively, you can use a contrasting thread color and topstitch around the entire coaster.*

**8.** Repeat for the remaining 3 coasters.

**9.** Host a BYOB party at your house, and don't stress about the safety of your new coffee table!

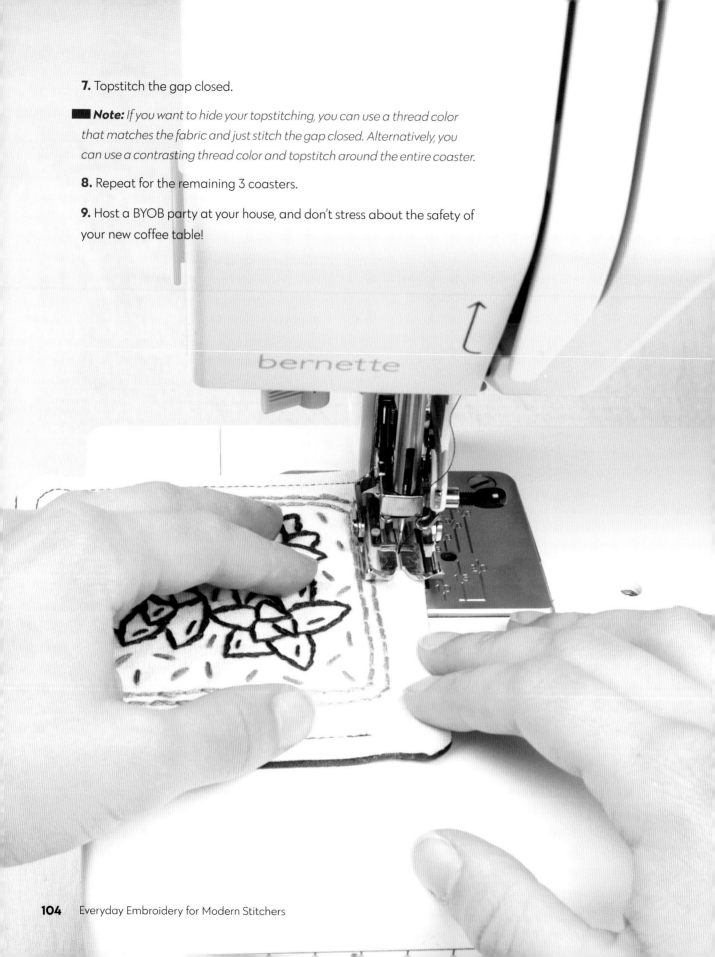

# MINI HOOP COLLAGE

FINISHED COLLECTION: 3 mini hoop sizes—55 mm (2.2″), 40 mm (1.6″), and 25 mm (1″)

Nowadays, everyone wants a gallery wall in their home. Why not make one out of mini embroidery hoops and show off your talent?

## MATERIALS

**Fabric:** 7½″ × 7½″ (19.1 × 19.1 cm) squares shot cotton in various colors

**Embroidery floss**

**5″ (12.7 cm) embroidery hoop**

**Mini hoop kits (by Dandelyne):** 55 mm (2.2″), 40 mm (1.6″), and 25 mm (1″)

**All-purpose craft glue**

## MINI HOOP SIZING FOR MINI DESIGNS

### Mystic Collection

**25 mm (1)**

Mini Tree Rune

Mini Bone

Mini Rune

**40 mm (1.6)**

Mini Feather

Mini Crystal

Mini Bird Skull

**55 mm (2.2)**

Mini Skull

Mini Shell

Mini Scarab

Mini Antlers

### Rockabilly Collection

**25 mm (1)**

Mini Anchor

Mini Star

Mini Diamond

**40 mm (1.6)**

Mini Cherries

Mini Heart

Mini Compass

**55 mm (2.2)**

Mini Swallow

Mini Key

Mini Cupcake

Mini Flower and Leaves

### Succulent Collection

**25 mm (1)**

Mini Ladybug

Mini Flower

Mini Leaf

**40 mm (1.6)**

Mini Bird-of-Paradise

Mini Succulent

Mini Potted Succulent

**55 mm (2.2)**

Mini Cactus

Mini Potted Cactus

Mini Close-Up Succulent

Mini Prickly Pear

# Embroidery

**1.** Select the Mini Designs of your choice (see Stitch Guides, pages 114–126) to fill your hoops.

**2.** Refer to Mini Hoop Sizing for Mini Designs (page 107) to order the correctly sized mini hoops.

**3.** Transfer your chosen designs onto the fabric, following the directions for How to Transfer a Design (page 14). Be sure to place your design in the middle of the fabric so you can use your 5″ (12.7 cm) embroidery hoop to sew it.

**4.** Place the fabric in the 5″ (12.7 cm) embroidery hoop. Stitch the embroidery however you like, or follow the Stitch Guides provided (pages 114–126).

## PREPARATION

Remove the embroidered fabric from your hoop, wash away any pattern marks or stabilizer, and iron your fabric, following the directions for Preparing Embroidered Fabric for the Next Step (page 25).

## ASSEMBLING THE MINI HOOPS

**1.** Follow the instructions for Mini Hoop Pinback Button, Assembling the Mini Hoop, Steps 1–5 (pages 85 and 86).

**2.** Repeat for the remaining hoops.

**3.** Arrange the collection on your wall, and hang the hoops with pins or brads. Step back and grin with pride!

**Note:** *Since it's going on your wall, why not hang an empty picture frame around the collage? It can then be the focal point for an even larger collection of embroidery projects.*

# DECORATIVE PILLOW

### FINISHED PILLOW: 12″ × 12″ (30.5 × 30.5 cm)

Add a little character to your favorite chair with a decorated pillow. This is a very quick sewing project, but it can instantly transform a den into a cozy getaway.

## MATERIALS

**Fabric:** ½ yard (45.7 cm) Japanese linen

**Embroidery floss**

**8″ (20.3 cm) embroidery hoop**

**Pillow form:** 12″ × 12″ (30.5 × 30.5 cm)

## STYLE NOTES

**Fabric:** Japanese linen in dark gray

**Embroidery floss:** Copper

## CUTTING

### Fabric

- Cut 1 square 13″ × 13″ (33 × 33 cm) for the front.
- Cut 2 rectangles 13″ × 9″ (33 × 22.9 cm) for the back.

# Embroidery

**1.** Choose the Antler or another large design (see Stitch Guides, pages 114–126) to stitch onto the front of the pillow.

**2.** Transfer your chosen design, following the directions for How to Transfer a Design (page 14). I used the tracing method to mirror the Antler design.

**3.** Place the front fabric in the embroidery hoop. Stitch the embroidery however you like, or follow the Antler stitch guide (page 117). I drew extra radiating lines in chalk to fill the space more. ⟶

**4.** Remove the embroidered fabric from your hoop, wash away any pattern marks or stabilizer, and iron the fabric, following the directions for Preparing Embroidered Fabric for the Next Step (page 25).

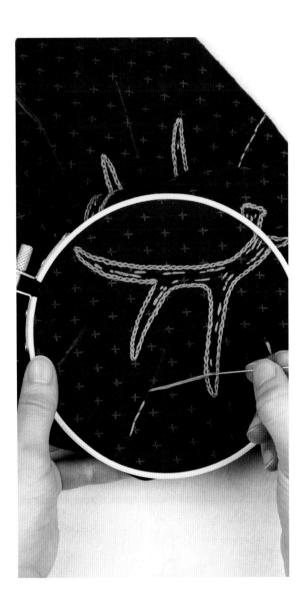

# Sewing

## PREPARATION

**1.** Lay one of the 13″ × 9″ (33 × 22.9 cm) rectangles down with the 13″ (33 cm) sides on the top and bottom. Fold up the bottom edge ½″ (12 mm) twice, and pin in place.

**2.** Using a ⅜″ (10 mm) seam allowance, sew across the edge to create a finished edge.

**3.** Repeat on the bottom 13″ (33 cm) edge of the other 13″ × 9″ (33 × 22.9 cm) rectangle.

## SEWING THE PILLOW

**1.** With the 13″ × 13″ (33 × 33 cm) square right side up, lay one of the 13″ × 9″ (33 × 22.9 cm) pieces on top, right sides together and with the raw top edges aligned. Place the other 13″ × 9″ (33 × 22.9 cm) piece on top of the stack, wrong side up, with the raw bottom edges aligned. Pin in place. ⟶

**2.** Sew a ½″ (12 mm) border around the outside of the stack.

**3.** Trim the corners at a 45° angle to remove extra fabric. This will make the turning easier and give you crisper corners. Make sure you don't cut too close to the stitching or the thread will unravel.

**4.** Flip the pillow right side out. You may need to use a pencil or chopstick to push out the corners fully. Insert the pillow form.

**5.** Pop the finished pillow onto your favorite chair and see how it instantly brightens up the room!

**Tip** If you want your pillowcase to be tighter, or if your pillow form is sparse in the corners, you can always flip the pillowcase inside out again and sew a smaller square ¼″ (6 mm) inside the first.

# STITCH GUIDES

The designs shown here are not true to size—a few are smaller, but most of them are larger. The actual dimensions are listed. Colors are suggested design choices. Feel free to select any thread colors you wish, or change stitch suggestions as desired. Make these your own!

## Mystic Collection

See Embroidery Stitches (page 18) for stitch instructions.

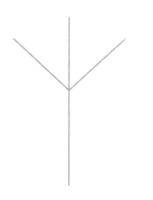

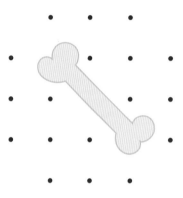

### MINI TREE RUNE

Size: ½″ × ¹¹⁄₁₆″ (1.2 × 1.8 cm)

— Backstitch

### MINI BONE

Size: 1″ × 1″ (2.5 × 2.5 cm)

— Backstitch

▨ Satin stitch

• French knot

See Mini Hoop Pinback Button (page 82).

### MINI RUNE

Size: ³⁄₁₆″ × ¹¹⁄₁₆″ (5 mm × 1.8 cm)

— Backstitch

## MINI FEATHER

Size: ¾″ × 11/16″ (1.9 × 1.8 cm)

— Backstitch

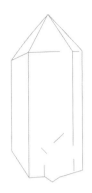

## MINI CRYSTAL

Size: ½″ × 1″ (1.2 × 2.5 cm)

— Backstitch

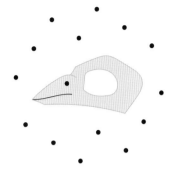

## MINI BIRD SKULL

Size: 1½″ × 1½″ (3.8 × 3.8 cm)

▦ Satin stitch

• French knots

— Backstitch

See Mini Hoop Collage (page 106).

## MINI SKULL

Size: 1¼″ × 1⅝″ (3.2 × 4.1 cm)

⋯ Backstitch

■ Backstitch to fill

See Mini Hoop Pinback Button (page 82).

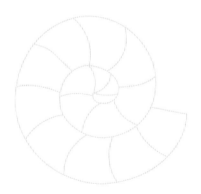

## MINI SHELL

Size: 1⅝″ × 1½″ (4.1 × 3.8 cm)

⋯ Stem stitch

See Mini Hoop Collage (page 106).

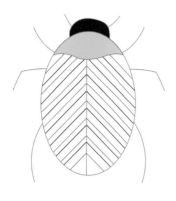

## MINI SCARAB

Size: 1³⁄₁₆″ × 1¼″ (3 × 3.2 cm)

 Satin stitch

— ▬ — Backstitch

See Canvas Shoes (page 36).

## MINI ANTLERS

Size: 1³⁄₈″ × 1″ (3.5 × 2.5 cm)

⋯⋯ Stem stitch

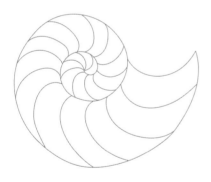

## AMMONITE (MEDIUM)

Size: 4³⁄₈″ × 3½″ (11.1 × 8.9 cm)

— Stem stitch

## TALL CRYSTAL (MEDIUM)

Size: 2½″ × 4⁵⁄₈″ (6.4 × 11.7 cm)

⋯⋯ Backstitch

See Half Apron (page 40).

## SHORT CRYSTAL (MEDIUM)

Size: 3¹¹⁄₁₆″ × 3″ (9.4 × 7.6 cm)

—— Backstitch

See Half Apron (page 40).

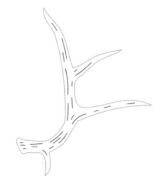

## ANTLER (LARGE)

Size: 4⅞″ × 4″ (12.4 × 10.2 cm)

—— Chain stitch

—— Backstitch

See Decorative Pillow (page 110).

## BIRD SKELETON (LARGE)

Size: 4⅞″ × 7¼″ (12.4 × 18.4 cm)

—— (crossing spine): Running stitch

—— Split stitch

## WINGED SCARAB (LARGE)

Size: 7″ × 6¾″ (17.8 × 17.1 cm)

— — —— Backstitch

See Lined Zipper Pouch (page 48).

# Rockabilly Collection

See Embroidery Stitches (page 18) for stitch instructions.

## MINI ANCHOR

Size: ⅝″ × ¾″ (1.6 × 1.9 cm)

— Backstitch

■ Satin stitch

See Mini Hoop Collage (page 106).

## MINI STAR

Size: ¾″ × ¾″ (1.9 × 1.9 cm)

— Backstitch

□ Satin stitch

• French knot

See Mini Hoop Collage (page 106).

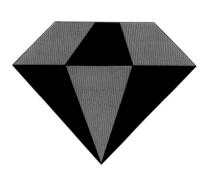

## MINI DIAMOND

Size: ¾″ × ½″ (1.9 × 1.2 cm)

— Backstitch

■ ▨ Satin stitch

See Mini Hoop Collage (page 106).

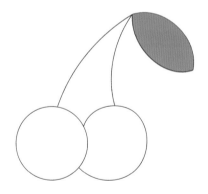

## MINI CHERRIES

Size: ⅞″ × ¾″ (2.2 × 1.9 cm)

– – Stem stitch

▨ Satin stitch

## MINI HEART

Size: 1″ × ¾″ (2.5 × 1.9 cm)

—— Backstitch

See Mini Hoop Collage (page 106).

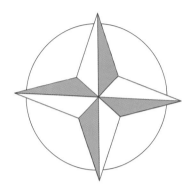

## MINI COMPASS

Size: 1³⁄₁₆″ × 1⅛″ (3 × 2.9 cm)

— — Backstitch

■ Satin stitch

See Mini Hoop Collage (page 106).

## MINI SWALLOW

Size: 1¼″ × 1¼″ (3.2 × 3.2 cm)

—— Backstitch

• French knot

See Fabric Cuff (page 76) and
Mini Hoop Collage (page 106).

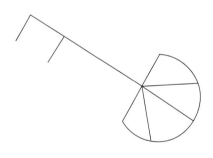

## MINI KEY

Size: 1⅜″ × ⅞″ (3.5 × 2.2 cm)

—— Backstitch

## MINI CUPCAKE

Size: 1″ × 1⅜″ (2.5 × 3.5 cm)

— Chain stitch

■ ■ Satin stitch

— — Backstitch

■ Backstitch to fill

See Mini Hoop Collage (page 106).

## MINI FLOWER AND LEAVES

Size: 1½″ × 1¼″ (3.8 × 3.2 cm)

— — Stem stitch

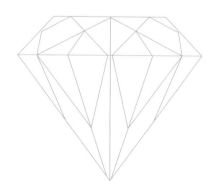

## DIAMOND (MEDIUM)

Size: 2½″ × 2⅛″ (6.4 × 5.4 cm)

— Backstitch

See Embroidered Cards
(page 66).

## STAR CLUSTER (MEDIUM)

Size: 2½″ × 2⅝″ (6.4 × 6.7 cm)

— Backstitch

## CHERRIES (MEDIUM)

Size: 2¾″ × 2¾″ (7 × 7 cm)

— — — Backstitch

• French knot

See Embroidered Notebook
(page 70).

## CUPCAKE (MEDIUM)

Size: 3″ × 4½″ (7.6 × 11.4 cm)

—— Chain stitch

—— Running stitch

—— Stem stitch

▨▨ Satin stitch

— — Backstitch

▨ (paper cup): Backstitch to fill

See Tea Towels (page 94).

## CAKE (MEDIUM)

Size: 4″ × 4½″ (10.2 × 11.4 cm)

—— Chain stitch

— — Stem stitch

—— Running stitch

▨ Satin stitch

See Tea Towels (page 94).

## ROSE (LARGE)

Size: 7″ × 4⅝″ (17.8 × 11.7 cm)

—— Chain stitch

▨▨ Backstitch to fill

See Jean Jacket (page 32).

# CRAFTER

## CRAFTER (MEDIUM)

Size: 5⁵⁄₁₆″ × 1³⁄₁₆″ (13.5 × 2.1 cm)

—— Backstitch

▨ Satin stitch

See Travel Coffee Cozy (page 62).

# Succulent Collection

See Embroidery Stitches (page 18) for stitch instructions.

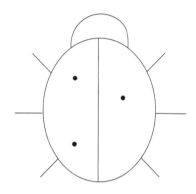

### MINI LADYBUG

Size: ⅝″ × ½″ (1.6 × 1.2 cm)

—— Backstitch

### MINI FLOWER

Size: ¹¹⁄₁₆″ × ⅝″ (1.8 × 1.6 cm)

—— Backstitch

### MINI LEAF

Size: ⅜″ × ½″ (1 × 1.2 cm)

—— Backstitch

### MINI BIRD-OF-PARADISE

Size: 1″ × 1⅛″ (2.5 × 2.9 cm)

—— Stem stitch

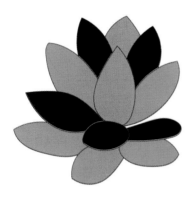

## MINI SUCCULENT

Size: 1″ × 1″ (2.5 × 2.5 cm)

—— Stem stitch

▨ ■ Satin stitch

See Mini Hoop Collage (page 106).

## MINI POTTED SUCCULENT

Size: 1″ × 1″ (2.5 × 2.5 cm)

—— Stem stitch

▨ ■ Satin stitch

See Mini Hoop Necklace (page 88).

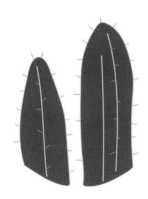

## MINI CACTUS

Size: 1¼″ × 1½″ (3.2 × 3.8 cm)

—— Backstitch

—— Running stitch

▨ Backstitch to fill

See Mini Hoop Collage (page 106).

## MINI POTTED CACTUS

Size: 1½″ × 1¼″ (3.8 × 3.2 cm)

—— —— Stem stitch

—— Running stitch

## MINI CLOSE–UP SUCCULENT

Size: 1¾″ × 1¾″ (4.4 × 4.4 cm)

⋯⋯ Stem stitch

## MINI PRICKLY PEAR

Size: 1¼″ × 1½″ (3.2 × 3.8 cm)

— — Stem stitch

● French knot

## GREEN SUCCULENT (MEDIUM)

Size: 3⅜″ × 3″ (8.6 × 7.6 cm)

— Backstitch

— Running stitch

— Split stitch

See Coasters (page 100).

## PINK SUCCULENT (MEDIUM)

Size: 3″ × 3″ (7.6 × 7.6 cm)

— Backstitch

— Running stitch

— Split stitch

See Coasters (page 100).

## TEAL SUCCULENT (MEDIUM)

Size: 3″ × 3″ (7.6 × 7.6 cm)

— Backstitch

— Running stitch

— Split stitch

See Coasters (page 100).

## GRAY SUCCULENT (MEDIUM)

Size: 3″ × 3″ (7.6 × 7.6 cm)

— Backstitch

— Running stitch

— Split stitch

See Coasters (page 100).

## SOLO SUCCULENT (MEDIUM)

Size: 3½″ × 3″ (8.9 × 7.6 cm)

— Split stitch

## POTTED ALOE VERA (LARGE)

Size: 3¼″ × 6″ (8.3 × 15.2 cm)

—— — Stem stitch

— ······· Running stitch

— Chain stitch

▦ Chain stitch

▧ Backstitch to fill

All yellow lines and fills represent white floss.

See Drawstring Bag (page 56).

## POTTED CACTUS (LARGE)

Size: 6″ × 8¼″ (15.2 × 21 cm)

—— Stem stitch

— ······· Backstitch

—— Chain stitch

# ABOUT THE AUTHOR

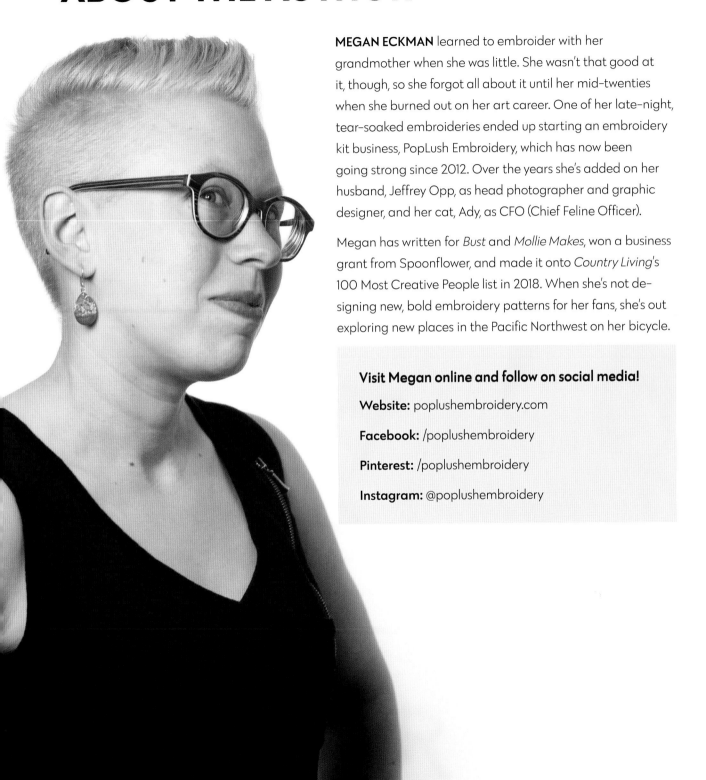

**MEGAN ECKMAN** learned to embroider with her grandmother when she was little. She wasn't that good at it, though, so she forgot all about it until her mid-twenties when she burned out on her art career. One of her late-night, tear-soaked embroideries ended up starting an embroidery kit business, PopLush Embroidery, which has now been going strong since 2012. Over the years she's added on her husband, Jeffrey Opp, as head photographer and graphic designer, and her cat, Ady, as CFO (Chief Feline Officer).

Megan has written for *Bust* and *Mollie Makes*, won a business grant from Spoonflower, and made it onto *Country Living*'s 100 Most Creative People list in 2018. When she's not designing new, bold embroidery patterns for her fans, she's out exploring new places in the Pacific Northwest on her bicycle.

**Visit Megan online and follow on social media!**

**Website:** poplushembroidery.com

**Facebook:** /poplushembroidery

**Pinterest:** /poplushembroidery

**Instagram:** @poplushembroidery

# Want even more creative content?

Visit us online at ctpub.com

**FREE PATTERNS | FREE VIDEO TUTORIALS | TOOLS | GIFTS & MORE!**

sew
snap
share